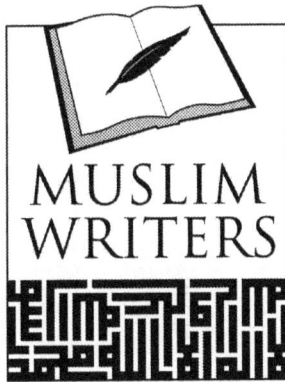

MUSLIM
WRITERS

Praise for the *Islamic Rose Books* Series

"I was pleasantly surprised to come across the *Islamic Rose Books* series by Sr. Delgado, a convert to Islam and accomplished and dedicated author. It wasn't just one well-written book, however, but four, so our eager young readers can continue to grow and experience life with the main character of the series, a young girl named Rose and her non-Muslim friends group called the Hijab-Ez, who take us on a journey of self-discovery as well as the discovery of Islam. We are presented with a number of very serious life moments and through engaging story-telling we are brought to realistic resolutions. The writing is terse, though not sparse, free-flowing, but not shallow. I, personally, plan to introduce these books in our Islamic school and also to donate them to our local library. Definitely recommend for your book shelves!"

- Yahiya Emerick, Author and Educator:
What Islam Is All About

"Linda Delgado has written an important book, one that demonstrates the willingness and ability of people of good heart everywhere to come together and understand one another. Through her lovable character, nine year-old Rose, the author takes you on a journey that is both touching and amusing as this young girl struggles to understand the beliefs and customs of a different culture and religion. This is a kind and gentle book that explores differences, yet illustrates what Douglas MacArthur said—that 'a better world shall emerge based on faith and understanding.'

As a Christian, I greatly enjoyed having many of my questions answered about Islam, and could not help but immediately read Book 2, *Friends*, which was a continuation of this delightful story about an American family's encounter with two police officers from Saudi Arabia. I highly recommend Delgado's books for young and old—they are impeccably written in a crisp style, tell a compelling story, and carry an important message about tolerance and compassion for all faiths. An outstanding book, and a must-read for all!"

- Andrew F. O'Hara, author of *The Swan*

"This books takes the reader through the roller-coaster mind of a nine-year-old. It's a treasure trove of information on Islam as Sophie's

World is for philosophy. A must-read particularly for children, young adults and just about anyone who's inquisitive about Islam."

- Neezam
Singapore

"Thank you, thank you, and thank you for the book!! What a pleasant surprise! You know what? I finished reading it in such a short time because I just couldn't put the book down! I really, really like your book, and I'm sure glad that it's published! It's really easy to read and I've no doubt that kids will love reading it."

- Hashima Mohd Hashin bom
Singapore

"I have forgot to tell you that I have finished book 3 and I am now on book 4 on chapter 7. When I was just about to find out what your secret was, I started to feel sleepy and I DIDN'T want to go to sleep. I really get excited when you and Rose say you have a PLAN. Your books are very interesting."

- Noori, living in the United Kingdom

Saying Goodbye

Linda D. Delgado

Muslim Writers Publishing

Tempe, Arizona

Saying Goodbye

Muslim Writers Publishing
P.O. Box 27362
Tempe, Arizona 85285
USA

www.MuslimWritersPublishing.com
and www.widad-lld.com

Library of Congress Catalog Number: 2005935795

ISBN 978-0-9767861-8-4
ISBN 0-9767861-8-4

Illustrations by Shirley Angum Gavin
Book cover designed by Zoltan Rac-Sabo
Interior design by A.P. Fuchs

Printed in the United States of America

Special Thanks

Special Thanks and love to my husband of thirty-one years, Raymond Delgado, a good cop, husband, father and grandfather.

Special Thanks to police officers Abdulraham AH Alwaily and Fahd Khalf Al-Harbi, from Riyadh, Kingdom of Saudi Arabia.

Special Thanks to Debora McNichol for her encouragement and support of my work.

Special Thanks to my friend and copyeditor, Pamela K. Taylor.

Special Thanks to my dear friend, Judy Nelson-Eldawy, for giving me permission to use the poems she wrote specifically for my books.

A Very Special Thanks to my dearest friend and author, Amatullah Al-Marwani.

**Bismillah Ar-Rahman, Ar-Raheem
In the Name of Allah,
Most Gracious, Most Merciful**

Dedication

Islamic Rose Books would not have been written without the Help of Allah and then the help, imagination and inspiration of my dear granddaughter, Cassy A. Tedla (my Islamic Rose).

Saying Goodbye

Table of Contents

Introduction — *Islamic Rose* Family and Friends

Rose—Leader of Hijab-Ez, ten-year-old only child, Christian background, mixed ethnicity, USA

Camelia—Member of Hijab-Ez, ten-year-old only child, Muslim, Egyptian-American

Ruby—Member of Hijab-Ez, eleven-year-old only child, Protestant Christian, Vietnamese National

Christina—Member of Hijab-Ez, ten-year-old with four siblings, Catholic Christian, Hispanic-American

Reyhannah—New Member of Hijab-Ez, ten-year-old with four older brothers, Muslim, Indian-American whose parents emigrated from India, USA

Grandma (Linda)—Rose's grandma, police officer, avid gardener, loves crafts, searching for truth about God, doesn't claim any religious affiliation, and believes in God but not the trinity, mixed ethnicity, USA

Grandpa (Ray)—Rose's grandpa, retired police officer, works evenings in security, Catholic Christian, Hispanic-American, USA

Dad (Tony)—Rose's father, single parent, lives next door to Rose's grandparents, Catholic Christian, mixed ethnicity, USA

Fahd—Saudi Arabian police officer, lives at Grandma's home for one year, Muslim, kind and smiles a lot, great story teller

Abdul—Saudi Arabian police officer, lives at Grandma's home for one year, Muslim, loves books and astronomy

Sylvia—Grandma and Rose's friend, owner of The Phoenician Restaurant, married to an Arab Muslim, mixed ethnicity, USA

Judy—Camelia's mother, Muslim revert, loves jewelry, co-owner of Casa Camelia Restaurant, married to an Egyptian, mixed ethnicity, USA

Definition: Hijab-Ez (pronounced *hijab-ease*) is a word Rose made up to identify the group of Muslim and non-Muslim friends who joined together to support her hijab-wearing school friend, Camelia. A member of the Hijab-Ez is a girl who wears a head covering regardless of her religious beliefs.

Prologue

Fahd and Abdul are Saudi Arabian police officers who came to the USA for one year and are staying at Grandma's house. They have successfully completed a six-month English course at Arizona State University and are attending advanced police training at the Phoenix Police Department. They continue to share their culture and Islamic values with Rose, family, and friends.

Ten-year-old Rose and her three friends are known at their public school as the Hijab-Ez because Rose, Ruby, and Christina wear headscarves each day to school to support their friend Camelia, who is a Muslim. During the first semester of their fifth grade year, the four girls have become loyal friends. They have met and overcome many challenges and their friendship has been tested. The diversity of their religious beliefs and ethnic backgrounds has united the four girls not divided them. During the second semester of the school year, the Hijab-Ez face many new challenges at school and with their families. The wisdom in the Islamic stories they hear from Fahd and Abdul, and family stories of the past, shared by family members, help Rose and the Hijab-Ez make decisions and solve problems.

Rose and the Hijab-Ez are about to learn there are many kinds of goodbyes. Saying goodbye can be casual—the kind where you expect to see someone again real soon. Then, there are the letting-go kind of goodbyes that often cause hurt and regret. Rose will soon learn that when another person says a different kind of goodbye and changes, her life is changed, too. The hardest kind of goodbye is the forever kind of goodbye that brings heartache and loss; but when faced with courage, sadness can be overcome, hope can triumph, and fond memories will remain.

1

Something Better

Rose was carrying a stack of freshly laundered towels down the hallway when she heard squealing vehicle tires and a blaring horn sound insistently. Rose put the towels on Grandma's bed and decided to go investigate. The commotion sounded like it was coming from in front of Grandma's house.

Rose put her hand on the front door knob, and jumped when she heard the three loud knocks and the doorbell ring. Rose called out, "Just a minute." She hurried through the house to the kitchen door, opened it, and called out to her grandma, "Somebody is at the front door. They knocked real loud and rang the doorbell."

Rose ran back to the living room and looked out the window. Her next-door neighbor, Mr. Gleason, was standing in the middle of the road next to a large blue car that was stopped in the roadway. A tall man with black-rimmed glasses was squatting down and putting something on what looked like a towel. Mr. Gleason and this man began walking towards Grandma's house. Rose saw a furry tail trailing from the edge of the towel. The furry tail was the same multi-color as Abu. "Oh, No!" Rose wailed aloud as she watched Mr. Gleason and the stranger approach the front porch.

Grandma hurried into the living room when she heard Rose's wail and was just in time to see Rose burst into loud sobs. The doorbell rang again, and Grandma opened the door. Mr. Gleason and the tall stranger stood there. The stranger cringed when he saw Rose standing next to Grandma with tears streaming down her cheeks. "I'm truly sorry. I put on my brakes, but I couldn't stop in time. The kitten ran out in front of my car. I think the kitten is hurt pretty bad and needs to see a vet right away."

Rose reached out to take hold of the bloodied towel holding her beloved Abu, but Mr. Gleason gently put his arm out to keep her from grasping the towel. "Abu is hurt, Rose, and we mustn't move him too much."

Grandma found her voice and said to Mr. Gleason, "Can you hold Abu and go with us to the vet's office?"

"Sure I can. Let me tell my wife where we are going."

"Rose, go get the car keys and my purse. Hurry now!" Grandma said as she looked at the stranger.

"Is it alright if I follow you to the vet's clinic? I would like to see what happens and help if I can. My name is Adam Harper and I live on the next street, 10th Street."

"I am sure you tried to stop in time. These things happen and sometimes cannot be avoided. Try not to feel too, badly. You can follow us to the Best Pet Clinic on Broadway. Do you know the location?" Grandma asked.

"I take my two dogs there for their shots and such," Mr. Harper replied.

Mr. Gleason returned and carefully took the towel with Abu from Mr. Harper. Rose, still crying silently, petted Abu's head as he mewed weakly. She looked at Mr. Harper and frowned, but didn't say anything as she handed Grandma the car keys. Rose and Mr. Gleason got into the back seat of Grandma's car. In less than ten minutes, Grandma pulled into the parking lot in front of the clinic. Mr. Harper parked his car next to Grandma's, and the three adults, Rose, and her injured Abu went inside the clinic.

The receptionist took one quick look at Abu, and then called the doctor on the PA system. Dr. Aimes hurried to the foyer where Rose was waiting with Abu and the grown-ups. Dr. Aimes motioned for Mr. Gleason and Rose to follow him to the examining room, while Grandma and Mr. Harper took seats in the foyer to wait.

Mr. Gleason placed the bloody towel and Abu on the examination table, and then sat in one of the chairs next to the wall near the doorway. Rose stood on the other side of the table and finally found her voice. "Dr. Aimes can you fix Abu? I think he is hurting awful. Poor Abu," Rose crooned to Abu as she gently stroked his ears.

"I don't know yet, Rose. Please sit next to your friend while Nurse Nancy and I have a look-see," Dr. Aimes said gently to Rose as Nurse Nancy steered Rose to the chair beside Mr. Gleason.

Mr. Gleason said softly, "Rose, I am going to get your grandma and I will wait in the foyer with Mr. Harper." Rose nodded her head, but didn't take her eyes away from watching Dr. Aimes and Nurse Nancy.

"Please God, don't let my kitty die," Rose whispered. Grandma came into the examination room and sat down next to Rose. She put her arm around Rose and pulled her close. Rose and Grandma sat silently together while they watched the doctor and nurse work on Abu.

Nurse Nancy left the room and returned with medicine that Dr. Aimes told Rose he was going to give Abu in a shot to help with the pain. Rose nodded her head and continued to pray silently. Time seemed to go by slowly. Finally, Dr. Aimes turned from the examining table and approached Rose and Grandma.

"Rose, why don't you go over and talk to your friend, Abu, while Nurse Nancy finishes cleaning him?" Doctor Aimes said in a kindly voice.

"Is he going to be okay?" Rose asked hopefully.

"I need to talk with your grandma a moment, and then we will talk about Abu's injuries," Dr. Aimes answered and motioned for Grandma to follow him out of the examination room.

In the hallway, Dr. Ames said very softly, "I am so sorry, but Abu's back is broken and he has suffered severe internal injuries. I cannot help him. He can stay here, so we can keep him comfortable until he dies, or we can put him to sleep. I recommend you give us permission to put him to sleep to ensure he doesn't suffer needlessly."

"You are sure there is nothing that can be done, Doctor?" Grandma asked, knowing the doctor would not have told her what he did, if there was any hope. Yet, she had to ask.

"No, I am very sorry. Do you want me to talk to Rose or do you want to do this?"

"I think Rose will accept that Abu will die if she hears you tell her and explain why he cannot be helped," replied Grandma sadly.

"What do you want to do for Abu?"

"I think we should ask Rose and see if she wants to make the decision. She can stay with him for a little while, can't she?" Grandma asked.

"I think we should allow a short time, and then, if she wants to hold Abu when I give him the shot, that would be okay. Abu will die very quickly and appear to just fall asleep."

Grandma nodded her head and told the doctor she was going to the foyer to explain the situation to Mr. Gleason and Mr. Harper.

Grandma walked to the foyer and explained that Abu could not be helped. She suggested Mr. Harper give Mr. Gleason a ride home as their waiting any longer would not benefit anyone. Grandma was concerned Rose might be angry at the loss of her kitten and speak inappropriately to poor Mr. Harper. He looked so distraught. Grandma assured Mr. Harper that he was not to blame and watched as the two men left the clinic.

When Grandma returned to the examining room, Rose was sitting on the examination table holding Abu. She was crying quietly and stroking his forehead. "Poor little Abu," she crooned to her kitten.

The doctor motioned to Grandma and whispered, "When I returned to the examination room, Rose seemed to know her kitten was dying. She asked me to help her kitty go to sleep. Rose told me that she watched Animal Hospital on television and knew how animals were put to sleep with a shot of medicine. I was quite surprised at how brave Rose is behaving. I gave the kitten the shot a minute or so before you got here."

Grandma nodded her head in understanding and went to stand next to Rose. "Shall we take Abu home and bury him, or have Dr. Aimes take care of this?"

Rose looked up with tear-swollen eyes and smiled wanly at her grandma. "We have to take him home with us, because Dr. Aimes doesn't have a yard here to bury animals. I don't want Abu to get burned up in the incinerator," she said matter-of-factly.

Nurse Nancy took Abu from Rose's arms and placed him in a clean, white wrapping and a large bag. Grandma steered Rose out the side door, and then remembered about paying the doctor. Nurse Nancy told Grandma that Mr. Harper had already settled the bill.

The ride home was very quiet. Grandma didn't say anything. She was waiting for Rose to speak. They arrived home to see Fahd and Abdul talking with Mr. Gleason. When Grandma parked the car, Fahd opened the back door and gently took the white bag from Rose's arms. "I am sorry, Little Sister," Fahd said gently.

Abdul shut the car door after Rose got out, and they all walked to the backyard. "I think we should bury Abu under the orange tree in the shady patch where the grass never grows," Rose said softly and looked at her grandma for approval.

"I think that is a good place for Abu to sleep," Grandma replied with a warm smile for Rose.

Mr. Gleason gave Rose a hug and said his goodbyes. His wife was waiting to hear what had happened.

Abdul went to the shed and got a shovel. He and Fahd took turns digging the hole for Abu. When they finished digging, Rose carefully laid Abu in the hole. "Wait a minute. I want to get a flower for Abu." Rose went into the shed, got the cutting shears, and cut a pink rose from one of the bushes next to the side wall. She laid the rose on top of the white bag covering Abu.

Rose stood silently beside Grandma as Fahd shoveled the dirt until the hole was filled. "Poor little Abu," Rose murmured softly, and then walked slowly to the back door of the house, and went inside. Grandma, Fahd, and Abdul went inside a few moments later to find Rose sitting in Grandpa's recliner in the family room.

"Honey, are you okay?" Grandma asked with concern in her voice.

Fahd and Abdul sat down on the couch, and Grandma sat on the arm of Rose's chair and waited for Rose to reply.

With a small catch in her voice, Rose spoke to no one in particular, "I asked God to help Abu, but Abu still died. The doctor couldn't help him. Why didn't God answer my prayer?"

"Sometimes God answers our prayers in ways we don't recognize or understand right away," replied Grandma.

"Your kitty would not be able to walk, if he had lived. He would not be able to jump and play, or get his food and water," Abdul said carefully. "Perhaps Allah knew this would not be good for your kitty?"

Rose considered what Grandma and Abdul said for a few moments. She turned to look at Fahd and asked him, "When I go to heaven will I see Abu?"

Fahd's eyes were so sad looking as he watched his "little sister" struggle to accept the loss of her dear little cat. He answered her question in a soft and soothing voice, "Allah has promised that we will be happy when we live forever in Paradise. If seeing Abu in Paradise is what will make you happy, then this would not be difficult for Allah to do for you. He is the Creator of all living things. Many times when we lose something we love, Allah replaces what we lose with something better."

Rose nodded her head slowly at Fahd. "It's hard to say goodbye to someone you love. I know Abu was a cat and not a person, but I loved him a lot because he was my friend."

"I know how sad you must feel right now, Rose. Remember that when God takes someone we love, He also comforts us. Be patient, dear, and please don't be mad at Mr. Harper. He felt so bad and he tried very hard not to hit Abu with his car."

"I know, Grandma. I am sorry now for looking so mean at him. Can I write him an apology note and take it to his house?"

"That would be very nice, Rose. Mr. Harper paid the bill at the hospital for us. It was very generous of him to do this. He has two dogs and he takes the dogs to see Dr. Aimes. Maybe we can meet his dogs?" Grandma suggested.

Rose nodded her head and said, "Grandma, I'm tired. I think I'll take a nap until my dad gets home." Rose looked over at Abdul and Fahd. "Thank you for helping me bury Abu." She stood up and walked slowly out of the room. Rose's shoulders and head were bowed as she walked to her study-playroom and quietly closed the door behind her.

∾

The next afternoon, Rose and Grandma were in the family room. "Grandma, do you think Grandpa will mind picking up Ruby and Christina tomorrow? Their parents said they could go with me to see Camelia in the play at the Islamic School." Rose tugged on Grandma's arm to get her attention. Grandma had been reading the Qur'an for the past hour, and Rose had been trying to read, too; but her thoughts wandered, first to her kitty, Abu, and then her thoughts went in another direction as she began thinking about Camelia's play tomorrow. She had difficulty concentrating on her own book and gave up trying to read anymore.

"If you ask him, I'm sure he won't mind," replied Grandma as she raised her head and pushed her glasses back up her nose towards her eyes.

Every time Grandma reads books, her glasses slip down her nose because she bends her head down while reading. I wonder if Grandma gets a sore neck from her head bobbing up and down. One of these days, I'm going to see her glasses fall off!

"Grandpa says you need some new glasses," Rose giggled.

"My glasses are just fine," Grandma sputtered indignantly, and then she had to laugh with Rose as she pushed her glasses back and raised her head to look at her smirking granddaughter.

"Did I tell you that Camelia's mom surprised Ruby and Christina? She gave them hijab scarves to wear tomorrow when we go to the play," Rose said happily.

"Your friends will be glad to trade in their handkerchief scarves for a real hijab scarf. You, Christina, and Ruby have been loyal to Camelia all year. I thought that after a few weeks the three of you would get tired of wearing the handkerchiefs each day at school, but I was proved wrong," replied Grandma thoughtfully.

"We are the Hijab-Ez! Friends forever!" exclaimed Rose.

The Hijab-Ez were a group of friends formed by Rose during the second week of school. Rose, Christina, and Ruby wore a handkerchief scarf on their heads each day at school to show support for their Muslim friend, Camelia. The Hijab-Ez were learning a lot about Islam through their friendship with Camelia and her family, and getting to know Fahd and Abdul.

The front door closed with a loud bang. Rose heard Grandpa talking to the door as if the door would talk back! "Alright, already," Grandpa grumbled.

Rose and Grandma looked at each other, and they both tried really hard to keep a straight face as Grandpa entered the family room wearing a huge scowl on his face. "I've fixed that door a hundred times, and still it closes with a bang. It's as if the wind just waits around, ready for me to open that door so it has a chance to slam it shut!"

"My, aren't we the grumpy one this afternoon. Did you have a bad day at work?" asked Grandma.

"Every day is a bad day when you have to go in to work on your day off," Grandpa mumbled under his breath.

"I heard that," giggled Rose. She couldn't help herself. Grandpa was usually calm and rarely raised his voice. It was unusual for him to be so grumpy about his work. "Grandma said you volunteered to go in to work today."

Grandpa looked sheepishly at Rose and Grandma, and replied, "You're right. I did volunteer when my boss called to tell me Joe was sick today. I shouldn't be so grumpy." Grandpa smiled at Rose and then hugged her and Grandma.

"Remember about Camelia's play tomorrow? Can we pick up Christina and Ruby before we drive to the Islamic school?" Rose looked up at her grandpa and added a sweet smile to her request.

"Didn't your dad say he would take you girls and then pick you up when the play was over?" asked Grandpa.

"That was the plan, but his boss called, and now my dad has to go in to work tomorrow because someone got sick. My dad didn't volunteer; he got told he had to go into work," Rose pouted as she finished her response to Grandpa.

Rose and her dad lived next door to Grandpa and Grandma. Rose's mother left when Rose was only a baby, and Grandma and Grandpa helped her dad take care of her when he was at work or away from their home.

"Now look at who is being grumpy," laughed Grandma.

Grandma, Grandpa, and Rose burst into peals of laughter. No one could ever stay mad for very long in Rose's family! Grandma and Grandpa exchanged glances. It was good to hear Rose laugh today. She was missing Abu, but trying very hard not to let her sadness prevent her from having other feelings. It was hard for Rose to say goodbye to Abu, but she was very brave and her grandparents were proud of her.

∾

Rose threw the covers off and jumped out of bed. Today was Camelia's play! Rose hurried to put on the special dress she had picked out the night before. The dress was long-sleeved, and the skirt barely touched the tops of her ankles. It was blue, like the color of a cloudless summer sky, and tiny, pink roses trimmed the high collar, cuffs, and the edge of the hemline. Grandma was going to braid her hair when she went next door after she finished breakfast. Dad was already up, dressed for work, and busy in the kitchen frying some eggs for Rose.

"Do you want one piece of toast or two?" Dad asked as Rose sat down on a stool at the kitchen counter.

"Good morning, Dad. One piece of toast is enough." Rose smiled at her dad as he placed the plate of eggs in front of her.

"You look real pretty in your dress, but your hair looks like a bird's nest," Dad laughed and poured Rose some orange juice.

Rose made a silly face at her dad, pulled a piece off the slice of toast, and dunked it into the runny egg yolk. In no time, Rose cleaned her plate and took the last gulp of orange juice. After a quick trip to the restroom to brush her teeth, Rose announced she was ready to go over to Grandma's house to get her hair combed and braided.

As Rose stood on tiptoe to kiss her dad goodbye, he looked down and said very seriously, "Remember, Rose, you are a Christian, and I don't want anyone at Camelia's masjid or school trying to get you to be a Muslim, you hear?"

Rose looked up at her dad's solemn face. "Don't worry, Dad. This is a kid's play, and only girls and women will be there. The play is at the weekend-school building. I won't be going to the masjid, and Ruby and Christina will be with me, too! See ya when you get home from work." Rose hugged her dad and then waited in the carport until he backed his truck out onto the street and headed off to work. *I wonder why Dad is always worrying about my Muslim friends trying to get me to be a Muslim. Maybe it's because Fahd and Abdul are Muslim and they are living at Grandma's house this year,* Rose thought as she walked across the yard and opened the front door to Grandma's house.

Grandma had learned from a flyer distributed by the local police department that police officers from Saudi Arabia were looking for American homes to board in while they studied in the USA. Fahd and Abdul were police officers from Saudi Arabia. Last Spring, they came to the USA to learn English at the state university and receive training at the city police department. Abdul moved into Grandma's house first, and then, a few months later, Fahd moved there, too. Rose and Grandma helped them learn English, and now Grandma was helping them with their police training classes. Rose was happy her grandparents decided to have Fahd and Abdul live at their home. Rose loved Fahd and Abdul, as they were so kind and funny. They sometimes called her Warda, the Arabic word for Rose, but mostly they called her "Little Sister."

"Grandma, Grandpa, anybody here?" Rose called as she walked through the living room towards the dining room.

"I'm in my bedroom, and Grandpa has gone to pick up Christina and Ruby," Grandma called out to Rose.

Rose walked back to her study-playroom and got her brush and hair ties for her braids. Rose loved spending time in her study playroom. Her grandparents had helped her redecorate the room last winter. Rose had chosen pink and lavender panel drapes to cover the only window in the room. Grandma had found a daybed at the second-hand store, and Grandpa had painted the wrought-iron frame white. Her bed looked like a couch in the daytime, and had pillows covered with the same purple and pink material as her window drapes.

Rose had tons and tons of stuffed animals, and they used to be scattered everywhere until Grandpa got a great idea. He built a shelf high up on each wall and Rose placed most of her animal friends on the shelves, which ringed the three windowless walls of her room. Her special animal buddies, like the unicorn, the teddy bears Fahd and Abdul had given her, and a white cat stayed on her day bed. Rose and Grandma had decided to build a bookcase for all of Rose's books and knick-knacks. They went to the lumberyard and bought six long boards and eighteen cinder blocks. The boards were stacked between the cider blocks, making six long shelves that ran nearly the length of one of the bedroom walls.

Dad had decided to join the redecorating project, too. He brought home an old wooden desk that was scratched in many places, but was sturdy and had two big desk drawers and a hutch that sat on top of the desk. Rose kept all her special stuff, like Jammie, her journal, in the top desk drawer. Grandpa had found some large colored plastic tubs that looked like barrels, and Rose stashed her skates, bicycle helmet, tennis racket, Frisbees, and other sports stuff in the barrels. Dad had even given Rose his old blue recliner so she could have a place to sit, relax, and read her books.

Grandpa had bought Rose a huge corkboard, which he mounted on the only wall in the room that wasn't covered with posters of animals. Rose used the board for tracking homework assignments and putting up cool stuff she found in newspapers or magazines. In the lower right corner, she pinned her monthly calendar. Rose liked to do her homework in her study-playroom because it was her special place filled with all her treasures.

Her favorite object in the room was the tall cabinet in one corner, which held her rock collection, which was stored in different sizes and colors of cookie tins. Next to her rock collection stood her telescope, which Abdul had taught her how to use to find constellations and planets on clear Arizona nights. Rose smiled as she looked at her recently cleaned sanctuary and turned off the overhead light.

She met Grandma in the hallway, and they both walked to the family room together. Grandma brushed Rose's fine golden hair until it shone, and then quickly made two braids, and pinned them at the top of Rose's head. Next, she helped Rose put on the blue hijab scarf Camelia's mother, Judy, had given her earlier that year.

Rose twirled around and asked, "How do I look?"

"Ready to go when Grandpa arrives with your friends." Grandma smiled at Rose as she twirled around the room. "If you're not careful, you'll make yourself dizzy!" exclaimed Grandma.

Just then, Rose heard the toot of Grandpa's truck horn. "They're here!" shouted Rose as she raced for the front door. Grandma hurried after Rose and watched as Rose climbed into the back seat of the truck. Grandma waved at Ruby and Christina, and smiled at the three young girls all dressed up in their long dresses and pretty hijab scarves. "Have a good time and say 'Salaams' to Camelia and her mom for me," Grandma called out to Rose and company.

"Hijab-Ez," Rose greeted her two friends as she fastened her seatbelt.

"I just love your dress," squealed Christina.

"Me, too," Ruby said more sedately.

"Wow! Your hijab scarves are really pretty!" Rose looked carefully at the new hijab scarves her friends were wearing. Ruby was wearing a green silk dress and a matching green hijab scarf that had small pearl beads trimming the edges. Christina was wearing a yellow chiffon dress with a matching hijab scarf that was a shade lighter in color and had small white daisies bordering its hem.

"I think each of you look lovely. You will feel very comfortable with Camelia's classmates who will be wearing hijabs." Grandpa smiled at the three girls, and then turned forward, and began backing the truck from the driveway. "See you later, Grandma!" the three girls shouted and waved excitedly.

In less than five minutes, Grandpa drove into the parking lot across from the masjid Camelia and her family attended. The parking lot was over half full, and more cars were entering as Grandpa parked his truck.

Rose gazed at the masjid in front of her. She loved participating with Camelia and her family in Muslim community activities. The masjid was so beautiful with its whitewashed walls and cobalt blue tile trimming. A gold dome and a slender minaret topped the masjid, giving it a beauty Rose could only feel in her heart, but could not find any words to express. A large, enclosed courtyard separated the masjid from a long, two-story building that housed the weekend Islamic school. Part of the building was still under construction. When it was finished, the Islamic school would be open for kindergarten through eighth grade for each school year. Part of the courtyard was filled with playground equipment, and several tall date-palm trees provided minimal shade for the benches surrounding the courtyard walls.

Rose looked towards the doorway of the Islamic school building and saw Camelia and her mother, Judy, waving at them. Rose also saw another young girl standing next to Camelia holding Camelia's hand. *Hmmm…I wonder who she is.*

Judy, Camelia, and the young girl walked across the parking lot to greet the girls and Grandpa as they piled out of the truck. "As-Salaam'Alaykum," Rose greeted Camelia, her mother, and her friend.

"Wa'alaykum as-Salaam," they greeted Rose, Grandpa, Ruby, and Christina.

"You three look very nice today. You did a good job fixing your hijab scarves in place," Judy said to the three girls.

Ruby and Christina thanked Judy for their gifts. Rose, Christina, and Ruby looked questioningly at Camelia and the girl standing next to her. "This is my friend Reyhannah. We are in the same Islamic class on Sundays, and our parents are good friends." Camelia smiled at her friend as she introduced Rose, Christina, and Ruby. "Please meet Rose's grandfather."

Reyhannah looked shyly at Rose, the gathered friends, and Grandpa, and said, "I am happy to meet you."

Judy and Grandpa talked for a few minutes while the girls walked towards the school building. Rose turned around and ran back to hug her grandpa. "Bye, Grandpa. I love you so much! And thanks for bringing us this morning."

Grandpa returned Rose's hug and said, "Judy just volunteered to bring you girls home. She is treating all of you to lunch at The Phoenician Restaurant. Grandma and I will see you later on this afternoon."

"Awesome!" Rose exclaimed and hurried back to her friends, who were waiting by the doorway for her return. As Rose approached her friends, she overheard Ruby asking Reyhannah if she had a part in the play. Before Reyhannah could answer, Camelia answered for her. "Reyhannah has one of the lead roles. She will be playing the part of Khadijah, and she helped design the stage decorations."

Rose narrowed her eyes and looked carefully at Reyhannah. She noticed that Reyhannah had very dark brown skin and almond-shaped eyes that were as black as coal. A few wisps of shiny black hair were peeking out from the red hijab scarf she was wearing. Reyhannah was wearing baggy red pants and a long, matching, red tunic top that had long, wide sleeves trimmed in gold braid. *Reyhannah doesn't look Arab and she doesn't look Mexican like Christina. I wonder what country or culture she is from*, Rose wondered silently. Rose watched as Reyhannah and Camelia held hands and walked in front of her. They entered the school building, with Ruby and Christina following them inside. Rose waited outside until Judy crossed the parking lot.

"I didn't know Camelia had a special friend. She never mentioned Reyhannah to the Hijab-Ez." Rose's lowered and subdued voice alerted Judy that Rose was a mite troubled about not knowing anything about Camelia's other friend, Reyhannah.

"Reyhannah and her family live in Mesa, and she attends another public school. Camelia sees Reyhannah at weekend Islamic school because this is the only school open for Muslim girls and boys. Reyhannah is Camelia's special Muslimah friend, and the Hijab-Ez' are her special non-Muslim friends. But you, sweet Rose, are her very special, I-haven't-decided-what-I-believe-about-God friend," Judy smiled at Rose and was relieved to see a slow smile light up Rose's face. "Reyhannah is a wonderful girl, and I am sure you will like her as much as Camelia does once you come to know her better," Judy said encouragingly.

"She does seem to be nice, and Camelia wanted us to meet Reyhannah. I am just being silly," Rose said sheepishly as she and Judy went inside to look for the other girls.

Judy and Rose found Ruby and Christina seated in the second row of chairs before a small stage. "Camelia and Reyhannah had to go back stage to make sure the props are ready," whispered Ruby as Rose sat next to her.

The stage was decorated with dozens of colored scarves hanging from the stage ceiling. A large, multicolored tent was erected on the right side of the stage, and a fake palm tree with colored pillows scattered before it in a circle were on the left side of the stage. A large silver banner was stretched on a rope or heavy cord across the top front of the stage. The banner had Arabic writing on it. "What does the banner say?" Christina whispered to Judy.

"The first line on the banner says, '*La ilaha ill-Allah*,' which means, 'there is no god but Allah (God).' The second line says, '*Allahu Akbar*,' which means, 'God is the Greatest.' The last line says, '*Alhamdulillah*,' which means, 'All praise is to God.'"

"Do you know what the play is about? Camelia wouldn't tell me," whispered Ruby to Rose.

"Remember the story about the wives of the Prophet that Fahd told me, and then I told you? Well, Camelia told her teacher the story, and they decided their play would be about the wives of the Prophet." On each chair was a paper that described the cast of characters in the play. "This paper about the play says that Reyhannah is reciting the part of Khadijah, the Prophet's first wife. Camelia told me that it is the longest part in the play. Camelia will be reciting the part of Safiyah. No one wanted to take this part because Safiyah was a Jew before she reverted to Islam and married the Prophet. Camelia volunteered to take the part of Safiyah," replied Rose.

"Don't the Muslims like the Jews?" asked Christina.

"I think it has something to do with the Israeli and the Palestinian people that have been fighting each other since Israel was made a country by the United Nations," whispered Rose.

Ruby and Christina stared blankly at Rose. Neither one really liked to study history, but Rose and her grandma were nuts-o about history. Just ask Rose a history question, and she or her grandma would know or find the answer!

"Shish! The play is getting ready to begin," whispered Judy.

The Islamic school teacher, Zaynab, stepped to the center of the stage and greeted the audience. Everyone called back, "Wa'alaykum as-Salaam."

"Today, the ICC Islamic School presents an original play titled 'The Wives of the Prophet.' Our fifth and sixth grade class created the script and set designs with the help of Allah and the writings of Muslim scholars. Please hold all applause until the play is over and all students appear together on the stage. I have been told that we have some guests today from outside of our Muslim community. I want to welcome each of you. We hope you will enjoy the play."

Camelia walked across the stage and stood in the center of it. She held a microphone in her right hand and began to describe the city of Mecca, which was the setting for the play. She was the narrator for the play, too. Each girl in the play took her turn walking to the center of the stage and, after introducing herself, recited the story of one of the wives of the Prophet.

When the play was over, the audience clapped loudly, and many women in the audience murmured "All praise be to Allah" and "Allah is the Greatest!"

Camelia hurried to where her friends and mother were waiting near the door. "Did you like the play? Wasn't it awesome?" Camelia gushed excitedly.

Judy hugged her daughter and smiled. "The story of the Prophet's (pbuh) wives is so wonderful, and you and the other students were outstanding!"

"Thanks, Mom!" Camelia hugged her mother and looked expectantly at her friends.

Rose, Ruby, and Christina grabbed Camelia and hugged her.

"You were wonderful," exclaimed Ruby.

"The play was great!" Ruby chimed in.

"Our hero!" added Rose with a big grin.

Camelia grinned back happily at her friends, and then noticed Reyhannah standing alone, a few feet away from them.

"Come join us, Reyhannah," Camelia motioned with her arm stretched out towards Reyhannah. Camelia lowered her voice and told her friends that Reyhannah's family could not come to the play today, so Reyhannah was just a little sad.

Camelia's Hijab-Ez friends turned and smiled at Reyhannah. "You were real good in your part, Reyhannah," Rose said as Reyhannah walked over and stood next to Judy.

"It was a good play, you two," added Christina with a friendly smile for Reyhannah.

Ruby stepped in front of Reyhannah and hugged her. "Your speech was the longest of anyone's and you didn't make any mistakes!"

A beautiful smile spread across Reyhannah's face and she stretched out her hands to the Hijab-Ez saying, "Thank you. I am so happy that you liked our play."

"We have to hurry now, girls. Reyhannah, Camelia, and I are going to get ready for prayer, and the three of you are going to wait for us in the school library. There are some interesting books for kids that you can look at while we are at prayer. We will only be gone for about thirty minutes. Will you be okay waiting in the library for us?" asked Judy.

Rose and Christina nodded their heads okay. "Can we go with you to the masjid?" asked Ruby.

"Not today, dear. I didn't get permission from your parents, but the next time I will be sure to ask for you," replied Judy.

Sure enough, in less than thirty minutes, Judy, Camelia, and Reyhannah came to the library to get Rose, Ruby, and Christina. Judy and her Hijab-Ez girls walked across the parking lot to the restaurant. Rose hung back and pulled on Camelia's sleeve.

"Why didn't you ever mention Reyhannah?" questioned Rose in a lowered voice.

"None of the Hijab-Ez knew her, so I didn't think to mention Reyhannah," Camelia answered, just a little defensively.

"I thought that you and I were best friends and we always tell each other everything," Rose said softly.

"We are best friends, and Reyhannah is also my friend. I was hoping you would like her, Rose."

"I do like her and she seems real nice," Rose answered quickly.

"Good! Now, if Ruby and Camelia like her, everything will work out great!" Camelia said and smiled at her best friend.

"I guess you liked Fahd's story about the wives of the Prophet," Rose said teasingly.

"Yes, I remembered you telling me Fahd's story about the Prophet's (pbuh) wives during the week I was gone on vacation for Spring Break. I told my teacher when she asked for ideas for our play, and she and my class thought telling the story was exactly right for us Muslimahs!" Camelia replied as she grinned from ear to ear at her friend.

"I'm happy to be of help. Just ask Rose!" Rose paused and took a know-it-all posture.

Camelia lightly punched her friend's shoulder and stuck her tongue out at her before quickly getting a serious look on her face. "Rose, I have something special to ask, so think first before answering." Camelia looked very serious. Rose was about ready to make a silly face at her friend, but immediately gave her full attention to Camelia when she heard her serious tone of voice.

"In a couple of days, Reyhannah's parents are going to move to a new house in our city. Reyhannah will be going to our school and the same middle school we will go to next year. She is going to be living in Ruby's neighborhood, too! I want to ask Reyhannah to join us as a Hijab-Ez. What do you think about this idea?" Camelia looked anxiously at Rose. After all, the Hijab-Ez had been Rose's idea.

"You really are soo…silly to be worried that I wouldn't want Reyhannah to join us," Rose gently chided her friend. "Of course, she can join us! I know Ruby and Christina will want her in the Hijab-Ez. Look at them walking up ahead of us. Already they are linking their arms with each other, and Christina is gabbing a mile a minute!"

"I told Reyhannah about us Hijab-Ez, and she thinks we are the cat's meow!"

"She likes cats, too!" exclaimed Rose.

"Reyhannah has two cats. They are longhaired, white Persians named See and Saw! See-Saw," giggled Camelia.

Rose gave a loud whoop when she heard this.

"Reyhannah is always telling me silly jokes. She has a warped sense of humor! Whenever I feel down in the dumps about something, I call Reyhannah, and she ends up making me laugh."

Talking about the cats made Rose think of Abu. Rose remembered what Fahd had said about God giving people something to replace what they have loved and lost. *I think God is giving me Reyhannah as a new friend to replace my kitty, Abu,* Rose thought as a warm, happy feeling seemed to lift her spirits and she smiled a truly happy smile.

"Look, your mom is waving at us to hurry up. When we go to the restroom to wash up, let's tell Reyhannah we have made her a Hijab-Ez, and we can teach her our friendship call," suggested Rose.

"Good idea. She is going to be sooo happy! I told her all about the things we do. She fell down and rolled on the floor laughing when I described the looks on the faces of the girls at school the first day you and Ruby put on your handkerchief head scarves and yelled Hijab-Ez as we walked by their group!"

"Well, she won't have to worry about trying to make new friends at school because she already has Hijab-Ez friendship. Come on, let's hurry because your mom is beginning to scowl at us," Rose urged. The two girls quickened their pace and caught up to Judy as she opened the restaurant door.

"It's about time, you two slowpokes!" exclaimed Judy. "The other girls are in the restroom, so hurry up and wash your hands, and then all of you meet me on the patio. I have reserved a special table for us, and Sylvia is going to be our special server today!"

Judy turned away from the girls as she heard Sylvia call a greeting to her. Judy looked back over her shoulder and said, "Now, don't stay in there all day. I'm as hungry as a bear, and Sylvia has made a surprise for you girls, so hurry up!"

Rose and Camelia opened the restroom door and were practically knocked down by Christina as she rushed over to them. Christina gushed, "Guess what? Reyhannah's parents are from India. She has four older brothers and is the 'baby' in her family. She has two cats named See and Saw! She is going to go to our school and…"

Ruby interrupted Christina's steamroller diatribe and said quietly with a serene smile, "and…she is moving to MY neighborhood! Look what she drew on my hand." Ruby pointed to the top of her right hand where a daisy was drawn. "Reyhannah said if she had her paints here, she could make it a yellow daisy. She used an eyeliner pencil she got from her mother to draw the flower." Ruby spoke with deep respect for Reyhannah's artwork. Ruby was an artist, too. She liked to create beautiful flowers and unusual shapes from intricately folded colored paper, and often decorated her creations with glitter and colored markers.

Rose and Camelia looked at their friends and just grinned in amazement. "What did you do, Christina, give Reyhannah the third degree?" Camelia asked and then giggled.

Christina looked kind of sheepish and shrugged. Ruby spoke up then. "We want to have Reyhannah join the Hijab-Ez. She knows all about us from hearing stories from Camelia."

"Super-de-duper! Camelia and I were just talking about this outside. Do you want to join the Hijab-Ez?" Rose asked Reyhannah.

"Yes! Yes! Yes!" squealed Reyhannah.

The girls quickly formed a circle and raised their right arms with their pinkie fingers extended. In unison they yelled, "Hijab-Ez! Friends forever!" The girls were so excited they laughed out loud, hugged each other, and began talking all at once. They sounded like a group of noisy birds twittering at the same time.

A head poked through the doorway of the restroom. It was Sylvia, owner of the restaurant. "You chattering magpies better hurry, 'cause Judy says there is going to be nothing left for you to eat but bread crumbs!" The girls rushed towards the doorway as Sylvia stepped aside and held the door for them.

"Do you know Sylvia?" Reyhannah asked Rose.

"Yep, she taught Grandma and me how to cook rice, right here in this restaurant. My grandma used to make rice that looked and tasted like glue!" Rose said and couldn't help but giggle.

The girls went to the side door of the restaurant, which lead to the patio area. They spied Judy sitting at the head of a long, decorated table, munching on some bread sticks. In the center of the table, dozens of colored balloons streamed from a large red and yellow decorated bowl. A red and white banner was strung up above the table and the words "We Are Proud Of You" were painted on the banner.

"Ruby, Christina, and I made the banner. Ruby drew the red roses on the border, Christina traced and colored the red and silver letters, and I bought the white banner paper," Rose said to Reyhannah and Camelia.

"Awesome!" Camelia and Reyhannah said together, repeating one of Rose's favorite expressions.

As the girls took their seats and Sylvia began bringing plates and bowls of food to the table, Camelia leaned towards her mother and whispered, "You were right. My friends really like Reyhannah and now she is a Hijab-Ez!"

Rose sat at the opposite end of the table and looked at Judy and her friends. She couldn't wait to get home to tell Grandma all about the play and her new Hijab-Ez friend, Reyhannah. Rose decided she would ask Reyhannah for the name of the city in

India where her parents lived before moving to the United States. Rose began to plan in her mind her research about India.

"Hey, Rose, stop daydreaming. Christina is going to eat everything–if my mom doesn't beat her to it–and you won't get any lunch," Camelia said jokingly.

"Beep! Beep! Earth to Rose! Earth to Rose! Fast food is fast disappearing," Reyhannah mimicked in the voice of a robot.

Rose blinked and looked around the table at her friends. She slowly raised her left hand, and in herkie-jerkie motions gradually dropped her arm and hand to her left side, and then promptly sat on her left hand. "Now, I am ready to eat!"

Christina, Ruby, Reyhannah, and Camelia copied Rose's antics. Judy burst out laughing. "Now that everyone has made sure they will use good manners while eating, can we please eat?"

The week following the play was a busy one for the Hijab-Ez at their school. They introduced Reyhannah to the teachers, and showed her where everything important was located–like their favorite spot next to the building wall where they met each day, the lunchroom where they usually plotted and schemed, the all-important restroom, and the lounge, so Reyhannah could say noon prayer with Camelia. Friday, at lunch, the girls made plans to meet the next day at Grandma's house. The Hijab-Ez tried to meet every Saturday morning at Grandma's house. This Saturday was going to be "special" according to Rose. She told her friends that a big planning session was needed, but didn't explain any further. Her friends were curious and, knowing Rose, when she said "Big Plans," they decided they better be sure and be at the meeting!

2

Summer Plans

Rose, Camelia, Ruby, Christina, and Reyhannah sat around the dining room table at Grandma's house. Rose was seated at the head of the table. She stood up and raised her voice, so she could be heard above the noisy chattering of her friends. "The Pre-Summer Hijab-Ez Weekly Group Meeting will come to order." Everyone kept talking, and Rose, looking exasperated, tried again. "Hijab-Ez! Friends forever!" Rose yelled and raised her right arm and extended her pinkie finger.

Her friends immediately jumped up and yelled back, "Hijab-Ez! Friends forever!"

"Now, that I have your attention, can we get down to the business of planning our summer activities?" Rose passed out pencils and three, blank, monthly calendar sheets to each of her four Hijab-Ez friends.

"Is the Big PLAN our summer activity planning?" Christina stammered indignantly.

"I thought we were going to do something special," Ruby added to Christina's complaint.

"If I told you we were going to spend Saturday morning doing this, you would have griped all week long about it," Rose fired back and looked straight at Christina.

Christina made a face at Rose and then smiled as she nodded agreement.

"What are we supposed to do with this?" Reyhannah whispered to Camelia as she pointed to the three blank calendar sheets in front of her. Today was Reyhannah's first Saturday morning Hijab-Ez meeting.

"Rose is our planner. You can count on her to plan just about anything and everything! She is so well organized that my dad says he'd hire her to run his business if she was old enough to work! If you got a problem, just tell Rose and she'll plot and scheme and worry it like a dog does a bone until she comes up with a PLAN!" Camelia whispered back while covering her mouth lightly with her fingers. She didn't want Rose to catch her talking when she was supposed to be listening!

"Well, that's a good thing for us, because my family says I'm a scatterbrain, and I joke so much that nobody seems to take me seriously in my house!" Reyhannah said petulantly and pursed her lips into a small pout.

"You're the baby of the family and, with four big brothers, you are spoiled rotten!" Camelia answered softly.

Almost at that same moment, Reyhannah and Camelia noticed that the room was awfully quiet. Only they were whispering, and, when they looked sheepishly at Rose, she was glaring back at them.

"If everybody is through having pri—vate conversations, can we get started?" Ruby and Christina covered their mouths and tried their best to smother their giggles. Soon all five girls were laughing, pointing fingers at each other, and making shish-ing sounds!

Grandma was standing in the kitchen doorway watching all the antics. She chuckled, shook her head, and made a beeline exit out the back door. *I wonder what mischief those urchins will plan for their summer meetings. I'll hear about their plans soon enough. I hope my surprise won't put a snag in the Hijab-Ez summer plans,* Grandma thought as she closed the back door and prepared to do some serious weed pulling.

Rose smothered her own giggles and said, "Now, if everyone is ready to listen, I will explain the blank calendar sheets I passed out to each of you. I am proposing that the Hijab-Ez meet every

Saturday during the summer months of June, July, and August. We can plan ahead for what we want to do on our Saturday get-togethers. This way, we will be able to let our parents know when we need their help with transportation."

Ruby raised her hand and began waving frantically at Rose.

"Yes, Ruby?" said Rose, just a tad annoyed at the interruption.

"Don't forget about the snacks…I mean, we need to be sure that we plan to have some good snacks!" Ruby said and nodded her head vigorously.

This started the girls giggling again, and Rose decided to change her tactics, so she waited patiently until they stopped giggling.

"Don't worry about the snacks, Ruby. I already included this in the "Summer Plan." The first thing we need to do is cross out on our calendar sheets the vacation days each of us will be away during the summer. I'll start and then we'll each say the dates we will be gone. Away from home…"

Rose – "Not going anywhere this summer."

Camelia – "Not going anywhere this summer."

Christina – "Not going anywhere this summer."

Reyhannah – "Maybe going to visit my relatives in India in August, but I am not sure."

Ruby – "Not going anywhere this summer."

"Okay, I think we can plan for June and July today, and, when Reyhannah finds out if she's going to India, we'll plan for August. Is everyone agreed?"

Rose's four friends nodded their agreement. "Each of us has a special hobby we enjoy, so I was thinking we could take turns showing each other our hobbies during our Saturday get-togethers. We could plan some field trips and check with our parents to see which ones could help us with the transportation to and from the places we decide to explore."

Christina had a slight frown on her face as she sat listening to Rose. *I think Rose has forgotten about my two little sisters. I don't think my mom can help cause she works, and I can't have meetings at my house when I am babysitting…this plan isn't gonna work for me!* Christina thought unhappily.

Reyhannah had her own worries about Rose's Summer Plan. *My mom doesn't drive. How will I get to everybody's house?*

Meanwhile, Ruby sat lost in thought, too. *My mom works every day, and I have to stay with my Aunt…and there is NO WAY my Aunt will let me invite four friends to visit me. She doesn't even let ME play in the house or outside!*

It seemed Rose and Camelia were the only two Hijab-Ez sitting at the table with happy looks on their faces!

Camelia looked at her friends and noticed the frowns on the faces of Ruby, Christina, and Reyhannah. She tugged on the sleeve of Rose's shirt and whispered, "Look at them. I don't think they are even listening to you. Something is wrong!"

"Hmm…I think I already know what the problem is for them," Rose whispered back to Camelia.

"Attention Hijab-Ez! I forgot to mention that my grandparents have already agreed that our meetings can be here. My grandpa doesn't work on Saturdays and said he could do the transportation part of the time and we can ask Camelia's mom if she will do the driving when my grandpa can't."

Ruby and Reyhannah began to smile, but Christina still had a problem. "What about my little sisters? What am I gonna do with them? Today they are with my aunt, but I can't count on my aunt every Saturday."

"I already thought about that. I asked my grandma if she would watch your little sisters for us when we have meetings and she said she would. She said she would go with us on field trips, so they can come with us. If everybody agrees to the Summer Plan, my grandma will call everyone's mother and get the okay. Any more problems before we get back to planning our meetings and field trips?" Her friends shook their heads. With a satisfied grin spreading across her face, Rose watched the relief flood the faces of her best friends.

Ruby looked thoughtful for a moment and said, "We have eight Saturdays and five talented Hijab-Ez. I propose we each plan one Saturday around our hobby and then we plan field trips for the other three Saturdays."

"Everyone agree with Ruby's idea?" Rose asked. Five eager hands were raised in the air.

"Let's have a picnic at the Tempe Town Lake Park for one field trip. We can take a boat ride on the lake, take our balls and badminton sets, and even bring our roller skates and skate on the skate-walk. The boat ride only costs twenty dollars a group, and I have enough saved from earning straight A's on my report card to pay the twenty dollars," volunteered Reyhannah.

"We could go to the Phoenix Zoo. My Uncle Lonzo works there and he can get us free, complimentary, all-day passes," suggested Christina.

Camelia was the next Hijab-Ez to speak up. "I suggest we go to the Phoenix Science Center. This summer there will be two different displays. One is about Astronomy and the other is about the History of Southwest Indians."

"Are there any more ideas?" Rose asked. They all shook their heads.

"Then I think the three field trip suggestions are approved. Any more questions?"

"I have a question. How much will it cost to go to the Science Center?" Christina asked softly. Her parents didn't make a lot of money and with Christina and four siblings, well, she wasn't sure if they would be able to give her the money for this field trip.

"Don't worry about that, Christina. I made straight A grades, too, and my money can is stuffed with dollar and five-dollar bills. I have enough for you, me, and everyone, and to buy treats, too!" Rose reassured her friend.

"I think any problems are solved, so let's plan on the three suggested field trips. Of course, we will have to get parent approval. OK?" All five girls nodded.

"Now, the next thing we need to do is to decide which Saturday each of us will present our hobby," Ruby said.

Now that they knew what they wanted to do during June and July, the girls discussed when they would schedule their activities.

For the next hour, the girls were busy completing the Saturday blocks on their June and July calendar sheets. When they finished, Rose read their Summertime Plan, just in case someone wanted to make any changes. She needed to give the plan to Grandma, so she could call all the parents.

"The Hijab-Ez Summertime Plan

June

First Saturday – Christina
Two-Stitch Embroidery: Christina will bring all the supplies for this hobby day – embroidery hoops, thread, needles, material, and a surprise pattern!
Second Saturday – A field trip to Phoenix Zoo before it gets too hot!
Third Saturday – Rose
Rock Hounding for Fun: Rose will show her rock collection and talk about places she has been to collect some of the rocks. She will use the computer and Internet to show different archeological sites people visit to see ancient writings on rocks and boulders. Afterwards, it will be swim time in the backyard pool, so everyone bring their swim suits.
Fourth Saturday – Camelia
Poetry, Rhymes, Books: Camelia will show the Hijab-Ez how to write rhyming poetry and limericks, and she will bring a list of great books for summer reading, plus summaries for some of the best on the list.

July

First Saturday – Field Trip to Tempe Town Lake
Second Saturday – Ruby
Arts and Crafts: Ruby will show the Hijab-Ez how to make animals and flowers by folding colored paper.

Other art projects will be presented for the Hijab-Ez to use their creative skills and imagination.

Third Saturday – Field Trip to the Phoenix Science Center

Fourth Saturday – Reyhannah

Body Painting: Reyhannah will demonstrate and then teach the Hijab-Ez how to use henna to paint intricate patterns and designs on their fingers and hands. Reyhannah will also talk about her parent's homeland, India, and bring a photo album of beautiful historical sites found in India.

Note: August – three weeks/meetings to be decided later."

Rose finished reading the schedule and asked, "Anything else we need to add?"

Reyhannah raised her hand to get Rose's attention. "Do you think that Fahd might come to one of the Saturday meetings and tell us some Islamic stories? Camelia told me about the neat stories he told the Hijab-Ez during the Spring Break vacation."

All four Hijab-Ez looked expectantly at Rose. They were surprised to see silent tears rolling down her cheeks!

"What's wrong? What did I say?" Reyhannah stammered in bewilderment.

Camelia replied in a hushed voice, "I forgot to tell you that Fahd and Abdul are returning to Saudi Arabia in three weeks. They are almost through with their police training. Every time Rose thinks about this, she starts to cry."

All four girls got up from the table, crowded around Rose, and began hugging her. "Don't cry, Rose. Look at us! Now we are crying!" Ruby managed to say. Her own voice broke as she offered words of comfort to Rose.

Christina broke away from the tight-knit group hugging and consoling Rose. She hurried out the back door to search for Rose's Grandma.

Grandma rounded the corner of the house and saw Christina hurrying towards her. "What has happened?" Grandma spoke with alarm when she saw the look on Christina's face. *She looks awfully upset.*

Breathlessly, Christina blurted out, "Rose is crying her eyes out because of Fahd and Abdul. Please hurry because we don't know what to do!"

Grandma dropped the garden hoe and exclaimed anxiously, "What has happened to Fahd and Abdul? I didn't hear the phone ring. Were they in an accident?"

As Grandma rushed towards the back door, Christina explained why Rose was crying.

"Oh, my goodness!" declared Grandma with heartfelt relief. "I think I almost aged ten years!"

When Grandma opened the back door, Rose was standing at the kitchen sink drinking a glass of water. "Are you okay, Rose?" Grandma asked with concern.

"Sorry I got everybody worried about me. I started thinking about Abu and then I got sadder thinking about Fahd and Abdul leaving. I'm gonna miss them so much. I wish they didn't have to leave."

"I'm going to miss them, too, but they are really excited about seeing their families again. It has been almost a year since they left Saudi Arabia." Grandma gave Rose a quick hug and asked, "Did you get through with your summer planning meeting? I was thinking you girls might like to bake some cookies and everyone could take some home to their family?"

"Bake cookies? Did I hear someone say bake cookies?" Christina poked her head around the kitchen doorway and grinned at Grandma.

In a second, the kitchen filled with chattering Hijab-Ez. Grandma watched Rose begin to smile and joke with her friends and knew the storm was over for the time being.

Ruby went to get the recipe book from the bookcase and was busy leafing through its pages when Grandma returned to the kitchen after scrubbing her hands. "Have you girls decided what kind of cookies to make?"

"It's my turn to choose, and I'm picking peanut butter cookies. Yum!" Ruby replied.

Ever the planner, Rose piped up and said, "We're going to need to make two batches to have enough cookies for everyone to take some home. Let's see, hmm…Camelia, Christina, and I will make one batch, and Grandma, Ruby, and Reyhannah can make the other one."

"Good idea. Otherwise, everyone will be running into each other in my kitchen," exclaimed Grandma with a chuckle.

Grandma, Reyhannah, and Ruby each got a glass of raspberry iced tea and went to relax out on the back patio, while Rose, Camelia, and Christina set to work making the first batch of cookies.

"Christina, you read the recipe and directions; I'll get the ingredients 'cause I know where everything is at in Grandma's kitchen; and, Camelia, you can do the mixing, okay?"

"We can all make the balls of cookie dough and flatten them with forks," chimed in Christina, who had been reading the recipe from the book Ruby handed her.

"Ready?" questioned Christina. Rose and Camelia nodded. "Let's begin!"

While the first batch of cookies was cooling on waxed paper on the kitchen counter, Grandma, Reyhannah, and Ruby mixed up the second batch. In no time, everyone was sitting at the dining room table, munching fresh peanut butter cookies.

"Mmm…!" was all anyone heard Ruby say as she stuffed cookies in her mouth right and left!

"Hey, Ruby, slow down! There won't be enough cookies left for anyone to take home!" teased Rose.

Ruby grinned at Rose as she brushed a pile of cookie crumbs from the table onto a paper napkin.

"I don't believe you for a minute, Ruby! You are even gathering up all the cookie crumbs to eat!" Camelia exclaimed.

Ruby looked indignantly at her friends, who were watching her careful progress with getting every last cookie crumb onto the napkin. "I was only cleaning up the mess I made," Ruby began sputtering until she heard her friends giggle and knew her friends were just teasing her.

"Grandma, are Fahd and Abdul coming home, soon? I was hoping Fahd would tell us a story before it's time for my friends to go home today," Rose calmly asked her grandma. Her friends each let out a sigh of relief. At least Rose wasn't going to burst into tears again!

"They won't be home until this evening. They are studying with their friends because final exams will begin Monday. They want to pass with the highest scores possible in their written exam and the practical police tactics examinations," Grandma answered as she headed for the kitchen, juggling the empty milk glasses in one hand and the tray of cookies in the other.

"We have another hour before Grandma takes everyone home. What do you want to do? We could play a board game," suggested Rose.

The girls were trying to avoid the backyard. Rose had told them about Abu getting hit by a car and dying, and they knew he was buried in the backyard. Nobody wanted to get Rose upset again.

"If your grandma says it's okay to use her computer, I can show everyone a real cool website I go to when I want to learn a new embroidery stitch. It tells you how to make the stitch, shows you step by step, and it even has pictures of patterns to use with different stitches. My relatives in Mexico make embroidered blouses and shirts to sell at the markets. I know another website that shows you how to make a weaving loom. My grandmother knows how to weave rugs and things. Last summer, she taught me how to weave a banner. When I got home, my dad made me a small loom – not like the big one my grandma uses – mine fits inside one of my dresser drawers." Christina paused to catch her breath. She loved to embroider and to weave on her loom. She got so excited talking about her hobbies that she ran out of breath!

Grandma overheard what Christina said and was already sitting at the computer when she called to the girls to join her. Christina told Grandma the website address to get to the embroidery web page. Grandma typed in the website address. In only seconds, "sharon b's Collection of Stitches for Hand Embroidery" web page popped onto the monitor screen.

Rose, Camelia, Reyhannah, and Ruby carried some chairs from the dining room, placed them in a half-circle behind Christina, sat down and watched as Christina explained the different embroidery stitches shown on the monitor screen.

"There are three stitches I use a lot. They are my favorites and easy to learn. The first is the 'Back Stitch.' It is one of the oldest stitches used in embroidery. You can use it for outlining and curved places on your pattern. The second stitch is really neat. It looks like a braid and is called the 'Pekinese Stitch.' Some people refer to it as the 'Chinese Stitch,' too. The third one is called the 'Cross Stitch.' It has many variations and is used on even-weave fabrics." While Christina described the embroidery stitches, she clicked web pages to show examples of how each stitch was made.

"It doesn't look so hard to do once you see the pictures," Reyhannah said as each of the girls took turns clicking on the names of embroidery stitches.

"I can hardly wait for summer and our weekly meetings. We are going to have so much fun learning how to do new crafts!" exclaimed Rose.

"I agree. I didn't think I would like learning how to embroider, but the pictures and explanations Christina just showed us have changed my mind. Now I want to get started!" Ruby chimed in.

"Another really neat website is the one I mentioned earlier where you can get free patterns. There are hundreds of patterns at this website. All you do is choose the one you like, click on the printer icon, and you have the pattern you want to stitch," added Christina.

"I know you are having fun, girls, but it is time for me to take each of you home," Grandma called out from the family room where she had been relaxing and reading.

"Just five more minutes, please! I want to show everyone the cool site that shows you how to make a weaving loom. We are going to make the loom and do some weaving when it's my turn to present my hobby at our summer meetings," Christina pleaded.

"Just five minutes, and then exit from the Internet and turn off the computer." Grandma walked to the living room and stood in the doorway watching the five girls. *Well, that's a first. Christina in the role of leader and the other girls quietly listening to her. I think the hobby meetings are going to give each of the Hijab-Ez the opportunity to lead and shine.*

❧

Grandma drove Ruby and Christina to their homes first. When they were nearing Reyhannah's house, Camelia nodded to Reyhannah and then cleared her throat. "Reyhannah and I have a small problem. We wanted to discuss it privately because we didn't want Christina and Ruby to misunderstand or have their feelings hurt. Christina suggested that after our hobby meetings we could all swim in your pool before our meetings end. I don't think Reyhannah's mother or mine will allow us to go swimming. My mom says you have to dress immodestly to swim, and that is something we don't do because we are Muslim."

Grandma stopped the car in front of Reyhannah's house and turned to look at the three girls sitting in the back seat. Reyhannah was nodding her head in agreement with what Camelia had just said about not swimming. Rose was looking at her two friends with surprise written on her face. *I know Rose wants to say something, but I don't think she knows what to say*, Grandma thought to herself.

"I will talk to your mothers about this. There won't be any boys or men at the house while you girls are swimming. I'll talk to Grandpa, and I know he won't mind spending the time next door while you girls are swimming. You wouldn't have to wear bathing suits. Perhaps you and Reyhannah could wear long pants and long-sleeve shirts that are old and which you wouldn't mind if they got faded due to the chlorine in the pool water?" Grandma saw the uncertainty on Camelia's and Reyhannah's faces.

"We don't have to swim. It's no big deal to me, and I'm sure Christina and Ruby won't mind either," volunteered Rose.

"Let's do this. I'll ask your mothers, and, if they say they would not like you to swim, then we will do something else. We can explain to Christina and Ruby. If they say you can swim, then I will explain to Ruby and Christina that there is a new fashion in summer swimwear. All of you will wear long pants and shirts when swimming!"

"And we won't have to worry about sun burns, either!" Rose said with a giggle. Reyhannah and Camelia started to giggle, and soon even Grandma was laughing.

"Reyhannah, tell your mom I will be calling about the summer plan," Grandma called after Reyhannah as she walked towards her front door. Next they drove to the Casa Camelia Restaurant where Camelia's mom was waiting for her. Camelia had to hurry, as it would soon be time for afternoon prayer. Grandma waved to Judy and called out she would telephone her later that evening. Judy nodded agreement and waved as Grandma and Rose drove out of the restaurant parking lot. The swimming plans were on hold until Grandma made some phone calls.

3

Graduation Day

Sunday morning was usually a busy one at Grandma's house. Fahd and Abdul were up early for Fajr prayer, and then they would be off to meet their police buddies for coffee and an early breakfast at the apartment of another Saudi police officer. Rose usually showed up around 7:30 AM, in time for breakfast and to see if she and Grandpa were going to church. Grandpa liked to fix eggs and toast for them each Sunday. He didn't cook much, but he had perfected his eggs-over-easy style—not one broken egg yolk or brown edges around the whites of the eggs!

This Sunday morning was different. Fahd and Abdul were sitting at the dining room table, drinking coffee, when Rose arrived from her house next door. Grandpa was in the kitchen fixing the boys their special kind of breakfast eggs. Grandpa was stirring the eggs in the skillet, adding onions, small chunks of fresh tomatoes, crushed red peppers, Hungarian paprika, salt, garlic powder, and cumin seeds. Rose watched as Fahd went into the kitchen, got the cinnamon spice from the cupboard, and added a dash of it to the mixture Grandpa was stirring.

Rose pinched her nose with two fingers, scrunched up her face, and uttered a loud, "*P-U!* That stuff stinks!!"

Fahd laughed heartily at Rose's expression. "This is very good, Little Sister. We are having some warm tortillas and some of Grandma's smashed beans. You try some?"

"You mean mashed beans," called Abdul from the dining room.

"The beans taste very good smashed or mashed," laughed Grandpa.

Grandma came into the kitchen from the back patio. "Good morning, Rose. Did you sleep well?"

"Yep, I slept like a baby," Rose quipped and smiled back at her grandma.

"What were you doing outside?" Rose asked.

"I was cutting some fresh flowers for the table. There are so many, and the roses are all blooming right now." Grandma was holding a large tray of roses. There were so many colors that they looked just like a rainbow.

"I'll get a vase for the flowers for you, Grandma. I don't think I want any eggs today. I'm going to have cereal and toast instead." Rose was certain she was not going to try the scrambled eggs that Grandpa, Fahd, and Abdul were going to eat.

After handing Grandma the flower vase, Rose went into the dining room and sat down across the table from Abdul. "I thought you and Fahd would be with your friends having breakfast. What's going on?" Rose raised her eyebrows and gave Abdul a questioning look.

"Rose, telephone your dad and ask him if he wants to come over and eat with us," Grandpa instructed Rose as he set the cereal, milk, and a plate of toast for Rose on the table in front of her.

"Okay," Rose answered cheerfully.

A few minutes later, Rose returned to the dining room. "Dad says to put the eggs and beans inside two tortillas and make him some burros. I'll take them over to him because he has to wait at the house for a phone call from work," Rose said as she snatched a piece of toast from the plate and took a quick bite.

"I didn't forget about my question, Abdul. Why are you and Fahd having breakfast here at home today?"

Before Abdul could answer Rose, Grandpa handed her a plate full of egg and bean burros for her dad. "Hurry back because breakfast is ready to eat," Grandpa said. Rose was already hurrying out the front door with the plate of food for her dad.

In a flash, Rose gave her dad his breakfast, a quick kiss, and ran back to Grandma's house. Rose slowed as she opened the front door and walked very fast (no running in the house!) to the dining room and sat down across from Abdul, again.

Grandpa, Grandma, and Fahd came into the dining room carrying plates of eggs, tortillas, and beans, and a pitcher of fresh squeezed orange juice. Rose waited impatiently for them to be seated before she said, "Abdul?"

"Little Sister, do you think we can eat first before I answer your question? I'm sooo hungry," teased Abdul.

Rose looked around the table and saw everyone trying hard not to laugh. *They know something that I don't know! Something is going on, for sure!* Rose thought.

Trying to act as though she wasn't all that interested, after all, Rose replied airily, "Nope, I don't mind waiting until after we eat. If it was so important, I am sure SOMEBODY would have told me already!"

Abdul relented, patted Rose's head, and said, "Tomorrow, Fahd and I will take the final police exam. Grandma is going to help us study for the exam today. Fahd and I are having a problem with understanding the justice system that is used in your country. After we pass this exam, we will be busy getting ready for our graduation ceremony on Wednesday. We have invited your family to come to the graduation on Wednesday morning. Afterwards, we are all going to eat lunch at the Haji Baba Restaurant."

"Wednesday? Wednesday! But, I have my district level exams on Wednesday and Thursday of this week. I have to take the tests or I won't promote to sixth grade. I can't miss them! Oh, no! I won't get to go to the graduation!" Rose wailed and looked crestfallen. Her disappointment showed in the droop appearing at the corners of her mouth and the suspicion of tears glinting in her eyes.

"Oh, Little Sister, I am so sorry. Abdul and I want you to come to the graduation." Fahd and Abdul looked just as disappointed and as sad as Rose.

"I will take the video camera and film everything, so you can see the video when you get home from school," offered Grandpa.

Rose sniffed and wiped the corner of her eye where a teardrop threatened to spill over.

Abdul thought for a moment and said to Rose, "Fahd and I will eat a very small lunch. We will save lots of room in our stomach for supper. We will go out and have a celebration supper on Wednesday evening. After supper, we can come home and see the video movie Grandpa takes. Fahd and I will explain what is happening in the video. Is this not a good idea, little Rose?"

Rose perked up on hearing Abdul's suggestion. She looked at her grandparents and Fahd. All three were smiling and nodding their heads in agreement with Abdul's suggestion.

Rose nodded her head, and a small smile began to replace the frown she had been wearing. "Thank you, Abdul. Your idea is super-de-duper! I love you. I love Fahd. I love everybody!"

Grandpa and Rose went bike riding so Grandma and the boys could have some quiet time for their study discussion. Fahd, Abdul, and Grandma quickly cleared the dining room table after breakfast and got down to work.

"Part of your exam will be to write a short essay comparing your justice system with my country's justice system, right?" Grandma asked.

"Right!" the boys answered in unison.

"We have had many discussions about your *Shari'ah* system of laws and Allah's justice," Grandma stated.

"This is true," the boys responded.

"I have an idea that might help you to describe and contrast the differences between the two justice systems," Grandma announced with an impish twinkle in her eyes.

Grandma got up and left the room. In a few minutes, she returned carrying two boxes. Box One was a five-hundred-piece puzzle, and Box Two was a one thousand-piece puzzle belonging to Rose. Grandma set the two boxes in front of the boys and announced, "The first box is your justice system, and the second box is my country's justice system!"

Fahd and Abdul looked surprised. They shrugged their shoulders and looked at Grandma with huge question marks in their eyes. They didn't know what to say, so they waited expectantly for Grandma to explain.

"Let's pretend that the name of the puzzle for Box One is 'The Muslim Way of Life' and the Creator of the puzzle is Allah. The directions for putting the puzzle together are the Qur'an and *Sunnah* of the Prophet. The rules for using the puzzle are the Shari'ah and opinions of the Islamic scholars. Mercy, justice, fairness, and truth are the four corners of the puzzle. What you see on the cover of the box is the puzzle put together correctly, and it is a beautiful picture!" Grandma finished her description and waited to see if her boys understood her explanation of Islamic justice.

"Ah-hah!" exclaimed Abdul excitedly. The question marks had disappeared from his eyes.

Fahd continued to look at Puzzle Box One and the question marks remained in his eyes.

Oh, dear. I hope I am not going to make things worse, Grandma thought with dismay.

Before Grandma could say anything else, Abdul turned to Fahd and said, "My brother, one of the pieces of this puzzle could be our prayer, another piece could be the Five Pillars, another could be punishment for sins, and yet another might be punishment for crimes! Do you see what I mean?"

Grandma looked anxiously at Fahd and was relieved to see his big, broad smile and the question marks in his eyes replaced by the gleam of understanding!

"Yes! Yes! It is clear to me now. So, one piece of the puzzle could be mercy for Muslims, another might be for halal foods, and another for good manners!" Fahd said with a voice filled with excitement.

"Each piece of this puzzle is made of a substance that can not be changed by anyone, just as Allah's laws cannot be changed." Abdul rubbed his hands together showing his enjoyment of this puzzle lesson.

"Sooo, we understand Puzzle Box One?" Grandma asked.

"Oh, Yes! This we understand, but what of the second puzzle box?" Abdul asked as he pointed at Box Two.

Grandma chuckled. "Box Two is also a puzzle. The title of this puzzle is 'The United States of America Justice System.' The creators of this puzzle are many different men and women who have lived during the two hundred and twenty-seven year history of the USA. There are many more pieces to this puzzle, too. Do you know why?"

"Is it because your people are always making or changing laws, so the size of the puzzle can change? There could be more or less puzzle pieces?" Abdul answered Grandma with two questions.

"Yes, to both questions!" Grandma was pleased with Abdul's reply. "The directions for the puzzle are all the laws in my country. Now here is where putting the puzzle together becomes confusing."

"How so?" asked Abdul.

"There are fifty big puzzle pieces, one for each state in the United States. Each of the fifty big puzzle pieces is divided into five medium-size pieces. The five medium-sized pieces have names. The names are: Federal Laws, State Laws, County Laws, City Laws, and, lastly, Other Laws."

"What is this 'Other Laws'?" Fahd asked with surprise.

"What is very tricky about the 'Other Laws' puzzle pieces is they are divided into many tiny pieces. The tiny pieces may have different names, and none are the same!"

"So, nothing is the same in each of the 50 big puzzle pieces?" Abdul asked in amazement.

"Well, each of the medium-size Federal puzzle pieces is the same in all the fifty big puzzle pieces," replied Grandma.

"Why?" asked Fahd.

"Because our Federal laws come from, or are linked to, the US Constitution and Bill of Rights, which were written by the men who created my country," replied Grandma.

"Is there anything else different about this puzzle?" Fahd asked.

"Hmm...yes, there is," replied Grandma. She watched the boys raise their eyebrows and shake their heads slowly. "The rules for this puzzle allow the fifty large puzzle pieces to grow bigger (more laws) or become smaller (eliminated laws). The judges in my country decide if laws are just. They decide what evidence is allowed in a trial. Our judges are the rules for Puzzle Box Two."

"Then your judges decide on how much truth will be learned?" asked Abdul.

"Yes," replied Grandma.

Fahd had another question. "Who are the people that write the laws? The men and women you spoke about?"

"Oh, they are elected, and their job is to write and pass laws. Ordinary citizens can write laws, too, and ask that their proposed laws be voted on in elections." Grandma waited to see if there were any more questions.

"When they write bad laws, we can say they are defects in the puzzle?" Fahd grinned as he posed this question.

Grandma and Abdul laughed loudly at Fahd's joke.

After Abdul stopped laughing, he asked, "Is this all we need to know about your country puzzle?"

"There are two other very important things to know. There are two rules that never change. Rule one says no one is allowed to write any law about sin. Rule two says that nothing about God is allowed to be in any law," Grandma said this very dramatically so the boys would understand the differences between the two puzzles.

Both boys looked indignant and then totally amazed when they heard this.

"Without Allah, I think your justice system will not be fair to people and will have many problems in it. Your people might have trouble deciding what is right and wrong, because right and wrong might change, just like the number of the puzzle pieces." Abdul's tone of voice was sad when he said this.

Grandma looked at Fahd and Abdul staring at the two puzzle boxes. "Do you think that my example of the two puzzles will help you to write your essay?"

"I will not have any trouble writing the essay, now. Thank you for helping us, Mum," Abdul said, and Fahd nodded his head in agreement. Abdul, and then Fahd, bent and kissed the top of Grandma's head. "We will go and get ready for Dhuhr (noon) prayer now. After prayer, we will study with Mohamed and our friends, okay?"

"That's fine, but don't be very late. Remember, your exam is in the morning," answered Grandma as she watched the boys go out the front door.

"Do you think the Muslim laws are better than our laws, Grandma?" Rose asked as she poked her head through the kitchen doorway.

"What? My goodness! You gave me a start, Rose! When did you and Grandpa get back from your bicycle ride?"

"My front tire got a flat, and we had to walk our bikes back. Grandpa is out in the patio fixing the tire. I came in and heard you talking, but I didn't want to interrupt," Rose answered with a guilty expression caused by having been caught eavesdropping.

Grandma ignored Rose's slip in manners and replied, "According to the boys, the Shari'ah are laws made by God and do not change. They are fair and just, and provide mercy equally to all people. Our laws can change, and are made by men and women. Justice is not always applied equally, mercy is not always considered, and religion is not permitted in any of our laws. The two systems are very different. I don't know enough about the justice system in Saudi Arabia to tell you if one system is better than the other. I do think it is important to consider that their system is based on laws and punishments created by God, and God doesn't make mistakes. Our justice system in the USA may not be perfect, but I think it is better than any other legal system that men and women have made for governing people."

"I can see why Fahd and Abdul were confused about how our laws work. I got confused listening to you explain!" Rose grinned impishly at her grandma.

"I suppose you are going to your room to write all this in your journal?" Grandma teased Rose.

"Yep, that is exactly what I am going to do," Rose called back as she headed towards her study-playroom to "chat" with Jammie, her journal.

❦

The following week, everyone was so busy that Grandma remarked more than once that time just seemed to disappear! Fahd, Abdul, and all their fellow Saudi police officer friends passed their final exams. Grandma and Rose picked out a special pen and pencil set for Fahd and Abdul, and had a verse from the Qur'an inscribed on the special case for each pen set.

Fahd's inscription read, "Who is better in speech than one who calls (men) to God, works righteousness, and says, 'I am of those who bow in Islam'?" *Qur'an 41:33*

Abdul's inscription read, "Glorify the name of your Guardian Lord, Most High, who has created, and, further, given order and proportion, Who has ordained laws, and granted guidance." *Qur'an 87:1-3*

Monday and Tuesday, the Hijab-Ez spent their recess and lunch periods talking about their summer plans. The Hijab-Ez could hardly wait for vacation time to begin!

On Wednesday, Christina brought a small weaving loom to school in her backpack and at lunchtime, she showed it to the Hijab-Ez.

"Wow! Did you make the loom yourself?" Ruby exclaimed when she saw it.

"My dad and I made it following directions we got from a real cool Internet website. It was so easy to put together. I'm going to bring the materials on my hobby day so we can each make a loom. Then, I'll show everyone how to weave using an easy pattern." Christina beamed. She was happy about the interest Ruby and her fellow Hijab-Ez were showing in the small loom.

Christina pulled a piece of weaving from her backpack. When she unfolded the cloth, the girls saw it was a banner and had the word Hijab-Ez woven into the center in bright green and yellow threads on a light crème-colored background.

Christina passed the banner over to Ruby, and then each Hijab-Ez took their turn examining the banner.

"I can't wait to learn how to weave. I want to make a banner with a picture of a cat in the center!" Rose spoke with such enthusiasm that the students sitting at the other end of the lunch table craned their necks trying to see what the Hijab-Ez were so excited about.

Christina was now fully warmed up on one of her favorite topics—weaving! "Ruby, I even found a website that shows you how to weave with paper! Yep, paper! I know how much you love to make figures and things from paper."

While Ruby and Christina chatted about weaving, Rose noticed how quiet Reyhannah and Camelia were. They hadn't joined in the conversation. When she looked at Reyhannah, Reyhannah's cheeks turned red, and she looked away quickly, pretending to be very interested in the half-eaten apple she was pressing between her hands.

Rose looked intently at Camelia. Camelia smiled back at Rose, but there was something funny about her smile. *It is like...well...fixed on her face... yea...her face looks like it is a mask! Something is big-time wrong,* Rose thought. *Maybe Camelia wants to talk to me without the other girls present?*

"I need to go to the girl's restroom. Do you want to come with me, Camelia?" Rose asked and looked pointedly at Camelia.

"Uh...no, Rose. I'm so hungry, and we've been talking. I need to eat my lunch!" Camelia stammered in response.

"Are you sure?" Rose raised her voice just a little and stretched out the word "sure," just in case Camelia didn't understand that she wanted her to go to the restroom.

"I'm sure," Camelia replied and took a huge bite of her sandwich, stuffing her mouth so full that both her cheeks bulged, making it impossible for her to answer any more of Rose's questions.

Camelia and Reyhannah's actions were now making Rose just a tad cranky with them. It wasn't like the Hijab-Ez to have secrets from each other or not share a problem. Rose really didn't need to go to the restroom, but she stood up, shrugged her shoulders, and went anyway. *I guess I'll have to call her tonight when I get home from school. Maybe by then, she will tell me why she and Reyhannah are acting so weird!*

Rose returned to the lunch table and noticed that Reyhannah and Camelia were now talking with Christina and Ruby about the weaving project Christina was planning for the group. *Hmm…maybe I was just imagining something is wrong?* Rose thought as she sat down at her place at the lunch table. Her friends were now looking at a piece of paper, and Rose held out her hand for Ruby to pass the paper down to her.

"What's this?" Rose asked as she looked at a graphic on the paper. It looked something like a spider's web.

Reyhannah looked at Rose, gave her a small, almost apologetic smile, and said, "It is a spider's web. Christina was telling us how we can make one by weaving it with yarn and a wire clothes hanger."

"Are we going to make one of these during your hobby day this summer?" Rose asked as she handed the paper to Christina.

"If we have time. I mean, I want us to make the loom and begin a pattern first," Christina answered.

"Talking about this spider's web reminds me of a story Fahd told me. One day, I asked Fahd what the Qur'an said about animals. He said bees, spiders, camels, ants, and birds, plus many other animals, are mentioned in the Qur'an. Fahd told me a special story about a cave, a spider, and a bird. He said a spider helped Prophet Muhammad by spinning a web in front of a cave where the he was hiding. A pigeon also helped by sitting in front of the cave. The bad men who wanted to kill the Prophet and his friend, who was with him, didn't check inside the cave. The spider and the bird made it look like no one had entered the cave."

"I know that story. The cave is named *Thawr*, and the friend who was with the Prophet (pbuh) was Abu Bakr. All the Muslims had moved away from Mecca—now called Makkah—to Yathrib, which is known as Medina, today. Allah gave permission for the Prophet (pbuh) to move because his life was in danger. This move is called the *Hijra*. The important tribal leaders and traders in Mecca didn't like the Prophet (pbuh) because the Prophet (pbuh) said that worshipping idols was wrong," Camelia finished the story Rose had begun.

"I want to make a spider's web!" exclaimed Ruby, Camelia, and Reyhannah in unison.

"Me, too," Rose chimed in.

"Well, it's settled then. A spider's web is what we will make on my hobby day!" Christina agreed, and she gave her four friends a huge grin.

"Oh! I almost forgot that Fahd and Abdul graduate today. Grandma and Grandpa went to the ceremony this morning. Grandpa is going to videotape it for me, and we're going to watch the video after we get back from having supper at the Haji Baba Restaurant tonight!"

Just then the bell rang, ending the lunch period, and Rose and her friends scrambled to clean up the lunch mess from the center of their table. "I'll tell you about it tomorrow!" Rose said to her friends as they hurried to get in the line forming for the return back to their classroom.

❧

When the last bell rang for school to end, Rose grabbed her book bag and hurried out of the classroom. She walked as fast as she could, waving all the time to Grandpa, who was waiting in his truck across the street from the school.

"Hi, Grandpa! Where are Fahd and Abdul? Where's Grandma? Did you have fun? Did Fahd and Abdul get any awards? What time are we going to supper?" Rose stopped her torrent of questions and gasped for breath. She was so excited she could barely wait for Grandpa to reply.

Grandpa mussed Rose's hair and tickled her under her chin. "Silly girl," he teased. "The boys went to a party the masjid is having for all the Saudi police officers. After they pray, they will come home and get us so we can all go to the restaurant."

Rose was just a tiny bit disappointed she would have to wait to see Fahd and Abdul. She understood they wanted to be with the other Saudi officers and receive the congratulations of the Muslim sisters and brothers at the masjid.

"Did they get any awards?" Rose asked a second time.

"I think I'm going to let the boys tell you all about the ceremony themselves. What do you think about this idea?"

"You're right, Grandpa. I'd much rather wait and hear Fahd and Abdul tell me about everything. Besides, we're gong to watch the video after supper, right?"

"Right," Grandpa agreed and started the truck so they could be on their way home.

~

Later that evening, Fahd and Abdul arrived at Grandma's just in time for them to go to the restaurant. During supper, Fahd and Abdul explained the graduation ceremony. The Chief of Police and the Training Commander were there to give each officer a certificate. A representative from their country's Embassy in Washington DC was also present, and presented each of them a letter from their King, thanking them for a job well done. They watched a video that showed the officers learning new skills, running, operating new computer systems, and practicing arrests. The funniest part of the video was the driver's training. Fahd said none of the officers wanted to drive fast. They had to drive fast on curving sections of a training roadway in order to pass the driving test. The instructor had to keep yelling, "Faster! Faster!" to each Saudi officer!

Fahd and Abdul both earned a ribbon and high honors for their skill in firearms qualifications.

Many of the other Saudi police officer friends of Fahd and Abdul were also at the Haji Baba Restaurant having supper. Fahd and Abdul left the table often to visit friends at their tables. The other officers came over to greet Rose and her grandparents. The Saudi officers thanked Grandma for the help she had given them during the past year. Rose was having such a good time she almost forgot to eat!

After supper, they went home to watch the video Grandpa had made of the ceremony. As Rose watched the video she thought, *Fahd and Abdul look so nice in their police uniforms. They are both wearing their new lieutenant bars. But I am going to miss them sooo much! I don't want them to go home to Saudi.*

It was very late when the video ended, and Rose had to quickly say good night to everyone and hurry home. She had school the next day. After she showered, Rose sat cross-legged on her bedroom floor and wrote some notes about everything that had happened during the day. It was only then that she remembered Camelia and Reyhannah's strange behavior at lunchtime. It was much too late to telephone either of them.

Rose sighed as she finished her notes, grabbed her hairbrush, and began tugging at the snarls in her long, damp hair. When she finished brushing her hair, she went into the living room to talk to Dad about the special supper and the graduation video.

When Rose finished recounting her evening, her dad said, "It's time for bed, Rose. It's late, and you still have a test tomorrow." Rose stood on tiptoes and gave her dad a big smooch as he bent down to hug her.

Rose got on her knees and folded her hands at her bedside to say her nightly prayer to God. "Thank you for bringing Fahd and Abdul into my life. Thank you for my good friends Camelia, Christina, and Ruby, and my new friend, Reyhannah. Thank you for my dad, Grandma, and Grandpa. I am sorry for all my sins, so please forgive me. Please keep my dad, Fahd, and Abdul safe, and let me see Fahd and Abdul again someday. Please help the sick and poor people, and help me be a good person. And God...help me find out what is bothering my friend, Camelia. Amen."

——— 4 ———

Disaster Strikes!

"Oh, my gosh!" wailed Rose as she threw off the covers and bounded out of bed. *It's 8:15 AM, and I've overslept! I have a test first thing this morning*, Rose thought with dismay.

"Dad! Dad!" Rose called out as she hurried into the living room. Dad didn't answer and he wasn't in the kitchen. Rose went back to her bedroom and quickly got dressed, dragged a brush through her hair, and called for a second time, "Dad!"

Rose rushed to the bathroom to brush her teeth and heard the back door slam. "Rose! Rose! Get up! You are going to be late for school," called Dad in a loud voice.

"Where were you Dad?" Rose asked as she hurried into the living room, grabbed her book bag, and headed for the front door.

"I'm sorry. I lost track of the time, Rose. I was changing the oil in my truck." Dad hurried after Rose, and they both walked quickly to Grandma's house.

Rose went through the front door, yelling, "Grandpa, where are you? I'm going to be late for school!"

Grandpa met Rose in the kitchen, near the backdoor. "Grandma was just going to telephone you to see why you hadn't shown up. Did you already eat some breakfast?"

"No, and there isn't time. I have a test first thing this morning and I can't be late!" Rose answered crossly.

Grandma came into the kitchen, opened the refrigerator, and took out a juice packet, a small baggie of white grapes, and an oatmeal bar. She handed them to Rose and said, "Eat these on the ride to school, dear. Calm yourself, too! You have enough time to get to class before the last bell rings."

Rose gave her dad and her grandma a quick kiss and followed Grandpa out to his truck, mumbling something about "...nobody is worried except me!"

As they pulled into the school parking lot, Rose noticed that the playground was empty. *I am really late and in trouble now!* "Bye, Grandpa," Rose said as she dropped the bag of grapes into her book bag and opened the truck door.

"Have a good day, Rose," Grandpa called after her hurrying figure.

❧

Rose got to her classroom, opened the door, and walked quickly to her seat. A moment later, her teacher walked in and began taking the morning attendance. *Whew! I made it just in time,* Rose thought as she glanced around her table. She noticed Camelia's seat was empty. Rose lightly kicked Christina's leg underneath the table to get her attention.

When Christina looked up with a startled expression, Rose whispered softly, but urgently, "Where's Camelia?"

Christina shrugged her shoulders, indicating she didn't know. Rose looked over at the next table where Reyhannah and Ruby were seated. Ruby was holding an envelope in her right hand and was waving it at Rose.

"Is there something you want to talk about, Ruby? What is in the envelope you are waving around?" Mrs. Rodriguez's voice dripped sarcasm. Mrs. Rodriguez hated to have attendance interrupted.

Ruby's face flamed brick red. She ducked her head, and quickly jerked her right arm down to her lap.

"Ruby!" called Mrs. Rodriguez. "Bring me that envelope!"

Ruby slowly stood and walked reluctantly to where Mrs. Rodriguez was standing behind her desk. Ruby placed the envelope in Mrs. Rodriguez's outstretched hand, turned, and, with her head hanging even lower, walked back to her desk and sat down.

Oh no! Rose wailed silently. *This day just gets worse by the minute! Now I've gotten Ruby in trouble,* Rose thought dispiritedly. Rose caught Ruby looking at her, so she mouthed the words "I'm sorry" silently to her.

Ruby blinked rapidly and gave Rose a smile that could only be called sick-looking. Ruby never, ever got into any problems, had perfect attendance, and was never tardy. The only time Ruby had gotten into trouble was when a bully threatened her, and everyone soon found out that Ruby hadn't done anything wrong. The teacher never scolded her for anything! Now this had happened, and during the next to the last week of school! *What else is going to go wrong?* Rose wondered.

Rose could hardly wait till the recess bell. She wanted to tell Ruby she was sorry again, and her curiosity about the white envelope kept popping into her thoughts as she tried to concentrate on the test she was taking. Rose also noticed that Reyhannah was very quiet. Every time Rose tried to catch her attention, Reyhannah looked away from her. *What is going on with my friends? Camelia isn't here, Ruby is acting strange, and Reyhannah hasn't looked in my direction, not once. Do I have cootie bugs or what!* Rose thought grumpily.

Finally, the recess bell rang, and Rose quickly headed for the classroom door. Before she could make her exit to the playground and her waiting Hijab-Ez friends, Mrs. Rodriguez called her to come back to her desk. *Now what?* Rose thought. *Maybe it's about the white envelope Mrs. Rodriguez took from Ruby.*

"I think this envelope belongs to you. It has your name printed on it." Mrs. Rodriguez held out the envelope to Rose. Rose took the envelope and stood waiting. "That is all, Rose. You can go to the playground for recess."

Rose walked as fast as she could without running, opened the classroom door, and then raced to the playground, where she found Ruby, Christina, and Reyhannah huddled in a tight group, whispering to each other.

The girls crowded around Rose as she tore open the white envelope. Rose read silently for a minute and then started to cry. Ruby took the note from Rose's limp hand and read the note out loud.

In the Name of Allah, Most Gracious, Most Merciful

Dear Rose and Hijab-Ez,

My babba (grandmother) in Egypt is very ill. Me, Mom, and Dad have 2 fly to Egypt 2 go and take care of her. I don't know when I will be back. Mom says we will probably stay all summer, maybe longer. Dad is not going 2 stay because of the restaurant.

My mom is going 2 call your grandma and see if you and I can see each other before we leave. We are leaving in three days and I have 2 help my mom pack.

I was really looking forward 2 our Summer Plan. I will write 2 you after we get 2 Egypt and I find out my address. Hey, maybe we could even send emails?
Tell Ruby, Reyhannah, and Christina that I will miss them 2 and hope they will write 2 me. I really wanted to learn how 2 weave. Maybe when I get back, Christina can show me! I have 2 hurry because Mom is taking this note 2 the school and bringing my final test home. I have 2 do it and mail it before Friday 2 the principal so I will get promoted 2 the 6th grade.

Don't forget me while I am gone… Hijab-Ez! Friends forever!

Camelia

All four girls began crying, but Christina was crying the loudest. Soon, her loud sobs caught the attention of the other three girls. They stopped sniffling, and Ruby asked gently, "Christina, is there something else wrong?"

Christina sobbed, "My mom and dad are getting a divorce, and my sisters and I have to move to Flagstaff with my dad! My brothers are going to stay here and live with my mom!" With a loud sob, Christina began to run towards the girl's restroom with her three friends running after her.

When they all got to the restroom, they took turns comforting each other, especially Christina. They each blew their noses and splashed cold water on their red-rimmed eyes. Finally, some calm settled on the four girls. Rose was the first to speak, "I am so sorry to hear about your mom and dad. Can I do anything to help you?"

Ruby and Reyhannah murmured words of sympathy while patting Christina's shoulders.

"I didn't even know my mom and dad weren't getting along. They sat us kids down in the living room and told us last night. My two older brothers got really mad at Dad. Mom and Dad said they both still loved us and...and (sniff).... that we would be spending time with both of them. Dad said they have agreed on shared custody! I don't want to be a shared custody!" Christina said loudly and angrily. "I want my family back the way it has always been!"

Rose, Ruby, and Reyhannah stood quietly with their arms about Christina as she cried and said angry words about things not being fair and how she was mad at both her parents. *I don't know what to say to Christina*, Rose thought in deep dismay.

"When are you moving to Flagstaff?" Ruby asked anxiously.

"My dad...sniff...sniff...said we are moving the week after school is out, and I am going to help him pack the things we will take from our house here." Christina hiccupped loudly, and three more hiccups followed. Suddenly, a small smile began to tug at the corners of her mouth.

The other Hijab-Ez started to giggle, and this seemed to make them feel just a little bit better. The end-of-recess bell rang. Rose suggested quickly, "Let's talk about this some more at lunchtime." The girls hurried out of the restroom and made it on time to the line-up for the return to their classroom.

Rose couldn't concentrate the rest of the morning. It was a good thing the class had taken the final test before the morning recess! All Rose could think about was that her best friend would be gone all summer, maybe longer, and Christina would be gone, too! Christina was so angry and hurt. Rose still couldn't think of what to say to her at lunchtime. *I sure wish my grandma were here right now, so I could talk to her*, thought Rose, sighing heavily.

The lunch bell rang, and Rose got up to join the other kids in line at the doorway. Mrs. Rodriguez assigned Jason to lead the group to the lunchroom, while she placed a gentle hand on Rose's arm and said quietly, "Wait here, Rose. I want to talk to you a moment."

After her classmates left the room, Mrs. Rodriguez asked Rose to sit down at a table with her. "One of the kids in class said Ruby, Reyhannah, Christina, and you were very upset during morning recess. Does this have anything to do with the envelope I gave you this morning?"

Rose felt so relieved to be talking to an adult that she poured out her heart about Camelia and Christina. Mrs. Rodriguez said, "Thank you for sharing with me, Rose. After lunch, I will take Christina to the school counselor, so she can talk to her about her anger. Reyhannah, Ruby, and you should just continue to be good friends to Christina, and perhaps you can stay in touch during the summer. I am very sorry you will miss your friend, Camelia, over the summer, Rose. You can go to the lunchroom now. When lunch is over, I will walk Christina to the counselor's office."

Rose thanked Mrs. Rodriguez, left the classroom, and headed to the lunchroom. Ruby, Reyhannah, and Christina were sitting at their usual table, talking quietly. "Is everything okay?" Reyhannah asked as soon as Rose sat down with them.

"No problem. Mrs. Rodriguez said one of our classmates told her we were upset and she was concerned, that's all. Christina, Mrs. Rodriguez is going to take you to the school counselor's office after lunch. I hope you aren't mad because I told her about your parents. You were so angry, and I didn't know what to say to you."

"That's okay, Rose. I'm not mad at you. I want to talk to the counselor. Right now, I feel like exploding. Maybe she can help," Christina replied and smiled wanly at her friend.

Rose turned her head and looked directly at Reyhannah. In a mildly accusatory tone of voice, she said, "You knew about Camelia yesterday, didn't you?"

Reyhannah's cheeks suddenly had two bright red spots of color. "I… I…"she stammered.

Ruby hugged Reyhannah and turned to Rose and said, "Don't be picking on Reyhannah. All she knew was that Camelia might be going to Egypt. It wasn't for sure yesterday. Reyhannah and Camelia overheard their mothers talking about it when they were at the masjid Tuesday night for the weekly Qur'an studies."

"I'm sorry, Reyhannah. I think all this sad news has got me churned up inside and not thinking right!" Rose said contritely.

Reyhannah nodded her head and went back to consoling Christina. Ruby sat quietly, gazing at nothing in particular. Her thoughts raced ahead. She felt panic as she thought about losing the company of her best friend, Christina.

Rose sat silently, thinking about Camelia and Christina. *At least Camelia would be returning at the end of the summer, but Christina was moving away for good! The Hijab-Ez just won't be the same without her. Our Summer Plan! It isn't any good any more. Everything is so haywire, now. Maybe Ruby and Reyhannah won't want to have meetings with just the three of us. What if their parents decide to go on vacation? Oh no! If that happens there won't be any Summer Plan—no meetings, no field trips, no hobbies, NOTHING…Nada...Caput!* These thoughts were just too much for Rose to deal with.

Mrs. Rodriguez approached their end of the table and spoke softly to Christina. Christina nodded her head, got up and followed Mrs. Rodriguez out of the lunchroom.

Rose watched Christina walk behind Mrs. Rodriguez. Her shoulders were slumped forward and her head was bowed. The sight of her heartbroken friend overwhelmed Rose with sadness. Her head began to throb, and she felt sick to her stomach. "I don't feel so good," Rose said to the two remaining Hijab-Ez. "I'm going to the school office and call home." Ruby and Reyhannah nodded to Rose and watched as she pushed her chair back, got up from the table, and walked quickly to the lunchroom monitor. "I don't feel well and need to call my grandma," Rose said.

The lunchroom monitor took one look at Rose's pale face and tear-stained cheeks, and, without a word, gave Rose a pass card for the school office where she could use the telephone.

When Rose got to the school office, she gave her pass to the receptionist and politely asked her if she could use the telephone to call home.

Ring! Ring!

Ring! Ring!

An out-of-breath Grandpa answered the phone. "Hello, who is calling?" he asked.

In a small voice, Rose said softly, "Grandpa, where is Grandma? I need to talk to her right away."

"Sweetie, Grandma is at her downtown office working right now. Is something wrong? Can I help you?" Grandpa asked with just the right amount of concern to get Rose's tears flowing again.

Rose said, in a tearful voice that seemed to crack and squeak, "Can you come and get me? I feel awful!"

"Are you in the school office?" Grandpa asked.

"Yes," replied Rose.

"I'll be there in less than five minutes. You wait right there for me, okay?"

"Okay, Grandpa," Rose said and hung up the telephone.

A few minutes later, Mrs. Rodriguez and Christina walked into the school office. Mrs. Rodriguez walked over to Rose and said, "The lunch monitor told me you would be here, and that you were going home. I hope you feel much better, and I'll see you tomorrow." Mrs. Rodriguez patted Rose's arm, and Rose nodded her head at Mrs. Rodriguez. Christina turned and waved at Rose as she and Mrs. Rodriguez went into the counselor's office and shut the door.

In record time, Grandpa was walking through the outer doors to the school office. When Rose saw him, she ran and hugged her grandpa around the waist. "Are you ready to go home?" Grandpa asked.

Rose nodded, and she and Grandpa left the school office and walked to Grandpa's truck.

The ride home was very quiet. Grandpa stayed silent and gave Rose time to speak when she was ready, but Rose didn't say a word. When they got to the house, Rose got out of the truck and hurried inside. She went straight to the message recorder on the telephone and checked to see if there was a telephone message from Camelia or her mom. There was one message from Camelia's mom, Judy, that said, "As-Salaam'Alaykum, Linda. Yes, Camelia can come over Friday evening and spend the night with Rose. We will bring her by the house after Maghrib prayer. Saturday, I will pick her up at 3:00 PM. Our flight for Egypt leaves on Sunday. Call me when you get home from work. Judy."

Grandpa watched as Rose rewound the message so Grandma could hear it when she got home. *Something more than Camelia leaving is bothering Rose. I hope she will decide to confide in me. Otherwise, I think I'm going to telephone and ask her grandma to come home,* Grandpa thought.

"Grandpa, I have a headache. I think I'll take a nap until Grandma gets home, okay?" Rose asked in a subdued voice.

"Maybe I could help you, Rose, if you tell me what is troubling you," replied Grandpa.

Rose ran into the family room and flung herself into Grandpa's favorite over-stuffed recliner. "Nobody can help this. Camelia is leaving Sunday and will be gone all summer. Fahd and Abdul are leaving in two weeks and they will be gone forever!" Rose gulped and continued, "The worst thing that happened today is Christina said her parents are getting a divorce, and she is moving to Flagstaff. She was sooo angry and upset today! I didn't know what to say to her, even!" Rose cried out in despair.

Grandpa scooped Rose up in his arms and then sat down in the chair. As he stroked her hair, he said, "This has been a very troubling day for you with so much sad news." Sigh.

"I don't know how I'm going to say goodbye to Fahd and Abdul in two weeks. Now, I have to say goodbye to Camelia and Christina, too. Grandpa, it just hurts so bad inside!" Rose burst into loud, wracking sobs. She cried and cried. Her heart and mind were filled with such sadness. Grandpa just held Rose and let her cry it out. Soon, he noticed that Rose's sighs and sniffles had stopped. He pushed back the long strands of silky hair from her face and saw that his Rose had fallen asleep, worn out from her tears and heartache. They sat there quietly, and soon Grandpa closed his eyes and fell asleep, too.

The front door shut with a loud bang. The noise startled Rose awake. She stretched and rubbed the sleep from the corners of her eyes. Fahd and Abdul walked into the family room just as Grandpa began to stir and open his eyes.

"What have we here? Rose is home sleeping when she should be in school?" Fahd teased. Then he noticed the dried tear-streaks on Rose's cheeks. "What has happened to our little sister?!" he exclaimed as deep concern filled his warm brown eyes.

Abdul dropped the packing boxes he was carrying and came to stand over Rose and Grandpa. "Why has our little sister been crying?" he asked softly.

Rose climbed out of Grandpa's lap, and the boys led her to the sofa, where they sat down beside her.

"Rose learned this morning that Camelia is leaving for Egypt to visit relatives for the entire summer and Christina's parents are getting a divorce. She got this news all at the same time this morning and did not know how to keep the sadness from spilling over while she was at her school," Grandpa replied to Fahd and Abdul's questions.

Rose sat silently, nodding her head up and down while Grandpa explained.

"My friend, Christina, was so hurt and angry at her parents when she told us about the divorce this morning. I didn't know what to say to her. Christina says that divorce is a bad sin according to her church, and she is so scared about this," Rose said softly.

"Christina's parents are Catholic, and their religion teaches that divorce is not permitted by God. Even if they divorce, their church will not recognize the divorce, and their priests will not perform a marriage ceremony if either one wants to remarry in the future," Grandpa explained to Fahd and Abdul.

"Christina says maybe it's her fault they are getting a divorce because she has complained a lot about having to babysit her little sisters," Rose added in a worried voice.

Grandpa said, "I don't think Christina has complained in a long time, now, has she? Not since the week your little cousin came to visit, and Christina learned how to get along with her little sisters, and learned all those fun things they could to do together, right?"

Rose nodded her head and looked slightly relieved.

"You could remind your friend about this, could you not?" asked Fahd.

"Yes...Yes, I think that would help Christina! What about divorce being a sin? What should I say to Christina about this?"

"I think the school counselor will talk with Christina today, and perhaps telephone her parents. They will probably go to the school and all talk together. It was a good idea to tell your teacher about Christina. She was able to help by taking Christina to the school counselor today," Grandpa said, and smiled at Rose.

Rose seemed to be calming down and becoming more relaxed. Grandpa, Fahd, and Abdul exchanged relieved looks with each other.

"Do Muslims get divorced? Do Muslims believe it is a sin?" Rose asked Fahd and Abdul.

Abdul cleared his throat and replied carefully, "Divorce is allowed by Allah. It is disliked, but permitted. Sometimes, when people are married, they begin to make each other very unhappy for many reasons. After they try to change what is causing them problems, if they still are very unhappy and cannot be kind to each other, Muslims consult their family first for help. When that does not solve the differences, the married people may go to the Imam at their masjid or an Islamic counselor for help. When they have tried everything, especially praying and asking for Allah's help, it is then that they may choose to get a divorce."

Fahd added, "When people get a divorce, this does not mean they are bad people. It means their marriage is not as Allah intended for it to be. The man and the woman should part as friends. If they have children, they should continue to care for them, and to teach them love and respect and how to be a good Muslim."

"Do you remember last year, when we talked about Camelia's cousin getting married, and what Fahd and I have planned for when we get married?" Abdul asked.

"Yes, I remember now. The man and the woman sign a contract to get married," Rose replied.

"They make promises in the contract. If they cannot keep the promises in the contract or live in harmony as Allah wants, then it is better to get a divorce," Abdul stated and looked at Grandpa, who seemed to want to add something to the discussion.

"Christina's parents are getting a divorce. Christina and her sisters and brothers will still have them as their mother and father. Their parents will still love them. The marriage is the responsibility of the parents and not the children. Do you understand what we have been saying, Rose?" Grandpa asked as he leaned forward in his chair and spoke directly to Rose.

"Yes, I think so. Christina's parents are getting a divorce, so they will not be mean to each other. Christina's parents will always be her parents, even after the divorce. Adults are responsible for a divorce and not kids. I can tell Christina how I live with my dad, and that I am very happy, even if I don't have a mom to see every day. If her parents divorce, she will still have her mom and her dad!" Rose looked at Grandpa, Fahd, and Abdul, and they each smiled at her. Rose smiled back at them.

81

Suddenly, her bright smile disappeared. Grandpa frantically searched his mind trying to think of something else he could say about divorce that would reassure Rose.

Raising his eyebrows in a questioning manner, Abdul glanced over at Grandpa.

Fahd squeezed Rose's hand gently and said, "I know why our little sister is still sad. It is because Abdul and I are leaving for our home in a couple of weeks. Am I right, Little Sister?"

Rose nodded her head, and a lone teardrop dropped off her small rounded chin. "What will I do without my friends? What will I do when you go home? I don't want you to leave. You are my only brothers. I'll never get to see you again, ever!" Rose's voice became a plaintive wail.

"Grandma will be home in another hour, Rose. Why don't we wait till she gets home and talk things over with her?" Grandpa suggested.

Rose nodded her head.

"Abdul and I will be very sad when we leave because we will miss you and your grandparents once we get home. Same as we missed our parents, family, and friends while we have been away from them. Insha'Allah, we will return to visit all of you. We can write to each other and talk on the telephone. You will write to Fahd and Abdul, Little Sister?" Fahd asked in his gentle voice.

Abdul added, "You will always be our little sister and we will never forget you, Rose!"

"I will always love you and Abdul, and I won't ever forget you, either. I will answer every letter that you write to me, I promise!" Rose flung her arms around Fahd first and then Abdul and hugged each one.

"Would you like to help us, Little Sister? Abdul and I brought many packing boxes home with us. Your grandma has given us so many things, and we must pack them to take home with us," Fahd asked.

"I'll help!" Rose answered with just a slight break in her voice.

"Good girl," added Grandpa.

"When we finish here, we must take many boxes to my friend's apartment. Fahd and I are going to ship these things to Saudi, so we can use them in our apartments at home," said Abdul.

"Yes, and your grandma bought me so many clothes that they do not all fit in my suitcases! I must ship them to my home, too. Your grandparents have been very generous to Abdul and me, and also to our brothers. We are grateful for this kindness we have been shown." Now Fahd and Abdul were the ones with big tears in their eyes.

"I think before anyone gets started with packing, we should all go get an ice cream. Who wants to go and get an ice cream?" Grandpa asked and waited expectantly.

"Me!"

"Me!"

"Me!"

Grandpa chuckled at Fahd, Abdul, and Rose's lightening quick response. They all headed for the front door and out to Grandpa's truck. Ice cream was just what Doctor Grandpa ordered for three, very sad, young people to cheer them up!

❧

When Rose, Grandpa, and the boys returned to the house, Grandma's car was parked in the driveway. Dad wasn't coming home tonight because he had to work the midnight to 8:00 AM work shift. Rose wished he were coming, because she wanted to tell him about what had happened today. *I won't tell him when he calls me tonight. He'll just worry*, Rose thought as she opened the front door and called out, "Grandma?"

"I'm in the kitchen," Grandma answered.

Rose went into the kitchen, Grandpa went next door to feed Rose's dog, and Fahd and Abdul went to their bedroom to begin packing.

"Are you real busy, Grandma? I have a lot of things to tell you. Did you play Judy's message about them leaving for Egypt?"

Rose asked in a rush. Grandma waited patiently to be sure Rose was finished speaking.

"I'm not busy, and, yes, I listened to my phone message, and, yes, I have time for us to talk. I put a roast in the oven with potatoes and carrots, so there is nothing else for me to do right now but listen to my best girl!" Grandma smiled and linked her arm with Rose's arm as they left the kitchen, walked into the family room, and sat down on the couch.

This time when Rose explained what had happened at school, she was much calmer. In Rose's gray-blue eyes, a hint of the emotional storm she had weathered still lingered. After talking to Grandpa, Fahd, and Abdul, the storm's aftermath left only a light mist of tears now clouding her eyes.

Grandma waited patiently for Rose to tell her about the discussion she had had with Grandpa, Fahd, and Abdul. When Rose finished speaking, she heaved a big sigh and looked at Grandma with a tiny glimmer of hope shining from those oh-so-expressive eyes. *Grandma always seems to be able to find a solution. Maybe she can help me figure out what I will do this summer without two of my Hijab-Ez friends. Grandma can probably tell me how I can help Christina, too,* thought Rose.

"Judy and I talked about how much you and Camelia are going to miss each other this summer. I didn't know about Christina, but our idea might help her, too."

Grandma watched as Rose straightened up from her slumped position, and she marveled at the rapt expression now spreading across Rose's face. *I hope our idea will appeal to Rose and help make things easier for her and the other girls.*

"Judy has found an Internet web site that is fun and safe for kids. At this website is a special page called Pen Pal Party. What you do is fill in a form that tells a little about yourself. Then the sister who created this web site will send you a name and password so you can join the party! There will be a list of pen pals for girls and boys. All of the Hijab-Ez can join and then email each other all summer long. Email is faster than snail mail, too. You can have fun at this web site by playing games and puzzles, and learning new things all the time. I found another website that is also safe for kids that has crafts and stories like the ones that Fahd is always telling you. This website even has words and phrases in Spanish, so you could begin learning another language. Sooo, what do you think of our idea?"

Rose's eyes shone as she thought about the possibilities—maybe she could meet some new friends from other countries! Rose's eyes clouded over when she thought of Christina. "What can we do about Christina? She will be so lonely in Flagstaff this summer. She won't know any kids."

"I think we can help Christina with this problem. Flagstaff is not so far from where we live. During the summer, you can call her once or twice a week and tell her about everyone else. You can also email her and have her join the Pen Pal Party before she moves. We can go visit Christina a couple of times this summer. It will be a lot cooler up in Flagstaff, and we can enjoy a few days there on each trip."

"Maybe we could go camping and have Christina and her little sisters go with us?" Rose said excitedly. "Maybe they could come and spend a week with me here this summer, too?" Rose asked hopefully.

"I don't see why not. We'll ask her dad before they leave. Christina may be moving to another city, but this doesn't mean that she will stop being your friend, right?" Grandma asked.

Rose nodded her head in agreement. "Your idea won't be near as much fun as the Hijab-Ez being together each week, but it is a pretty good idea," Rose said with a big smile to let Grandma know that she liked and appreciated her ideas.

"Oh, there is one more thing I forgot to tell you. Remember those field trips you girls were going to take? Well, Reyhannah, Ruby and you can still go on them, and you can tell Christina and Camelia all about the field trips in your emails," Grandma added.

"Thanks, Grandma. I can always count on you!" Rose exclaimed.

"Well, now that we kinda have things settled about summer vacation, have you done any thinking about what you and Camelia want to do tomorrow and Saturday? Did you telephone her and ask what she might like to do? This is the very first time her father has allowed her to stay overnight with anyone other than her family. We must make sure Camelia remembers her prayer times, okay?" Grandma asked.

"Okay. Can I call her now and see what she has in mind?" Rose asked.

"Sure, just don't stay on the line for very long, as they might be waiting to hear news about Camelia's grandmother."

"I'll only talk a few minutes, promise," replied Rose as she went to the living room to make her telephone call.

A few minutes later, Rose called out to Grandma, "Can Camelia and I use your computer tomorrow? We want to sign up for the Pen Pal Party thingy. I can tell Ruby, Reyhannah, and Christina about it tomorrow at school."

"Of course, you and Camelia can use my computer. Just remember the rule."

"I know, I know, don't go to another website without asking first," Rose answered.

Grandma smiled and was relieved to see Rose's usual sunny nature resurface once again. *Grandpa and the boys must have had their hands full this afternoon. They did a great job helping Rose through her emotional storm,* Grandma thought as she walked to the kitchen to check on the roast in the oven.

Rose rejoined her grandma in the kitchen. "Tomorrow, Camelia wants us to research Egypt on the Internet. She visited her dad's family twice, but she was too small and doesn't remember that much. Oh, Judy said to tell you the surgery for her mother-in-law is scheduled for next Tuesday. Camelia and her parents will already be in Egypt then. She also said not to cook tomorrow. When they bring Camelia, they are going to bring us supper! Mmm!! I just love Italian food. I hope they bring me spaghetti!"

"You didn't happen to say anything about spaghetti when you talked to Judy, did you?" Grandma teased.

"Nope, I didn't, because Camelia did that for me!" Rose grinned back impishly.

Fahd and Abdul walked into the kitchen, and Abdul said, "We're going now, Mum." Fahd and Abdul kissed the top of

Grandma's head and then hugged Rose. "We will be out late, so don't wait up, please. Maybe we will spend the night at the apartment as we have much to do and many phone calls to make to our families. We will see you tomorrow after Jumu'ah prayer, Little Sister."

"Be careful," Grandma called after her boys.

"See you later, al-li-gator!" called Rose.

"After while croc-o-dile," Fahd called back with a laugh!

Rose beamed a smile at Fahd. He finally said it right!

❧

Monday morning, Rose climbed into the truck, fastened her seat belt, and stared straight ahead. Her thoughts were not about today or school. Last week had been the worst week that Rose could remember in her entire life. The week ended with Rose and her grandparents taking Camelia and her parents to the airport for their trip to Egypt. Saying goodbye to Camelia had been very hard, and both girls cried buckets of tears. Now, this week, she had to say goodbye to her other Hijab-Ez friend, Christina.

Grandpa looked over at Rose and noticed her preoccupied silence. Trying to cheer her up, he said, "Wasn't it a nice surprise when Ruby, Reyhannah, and Christina arrived Saturday morning? When they came through the front door, you girls began jumping up and down, squealing, laughing, and hugging each other. You sounded like one hundred people, not five girls!" Grandpa teased.

Rose smiled absentmindedly, nodded her head at Grandpa, and drifted back to remembering the weekend she had shared with her friends...

Friday evening, Camelia had arrived with a ton of spaghetti, green salad, and hot, buttered garlic bread. They had spent most of the evening researching Egypt using Grandma's computer. Camelia's grandmother lived in a small rural village in northeast Egypt, just two hundred miles from the Gaza Strip and Israel. The village name was *Saft Turab*. It is pronounced "soft drub," but the name means dirt! Rose and Camelia had both giggled about naming a town Dirt! It seemed like an unusual name to give a town.

Saturday was a day Rose would long remember! Grandma had located the "We Love Islam" web site, and each of the girls had joined the Pen Pal Party. Christina had told her Hijab-Ez friends that her parents had come to the school counselor's office, and they had had a long talk with the counselor. She was still very upset about her parents getting a divorce, but Rose thought she wasn't so angry anymore. *Thank God for this,* Rose had thought.

Christina had surprised them by bringing wire coat hangers and dozens of different-colored bundles of yarn. They had spent a couple of hours making the spider webs Christina had told them about during one of their lunch hours at school. She had also showed them the websites for embroidery and the special one that showed how to make a loom for weaving.

When it was time for everyone to go home on Saturday afternoon, the girls had hugged and cried and promised to write each other. Christina had cried the most, because she would not be coming back at the end of summer to be with her Hijab-Ez friends the next school year.

Sunday, while they were at the airport waiting for the plane's departure time, Judy had told Camelia and Rose more about the town where Camelia and her mother would be living during the summer months. Judy had said that the town was very small and only had dirt roads with deep ruts in them. Every morning and evening, people drove cows, water buffalo, sheep, and goats through the main street. Chickens, geese, and ducks ran wild everywhere, too. The main street was lined with vegetable stands, fresh meat stalls, trinket shops, cloth stalls, and bakeries. People didn't use clothes dryers, but hung their laundry on metal racks placed on roof balconies.

Judy had said that Egypt and the small town were very noisy. There were kids playing in the streets, people reciting Qur'an, tradespeople calling out to people passing by, and animals everywhere. The strangest thing she had told them was about bathrooms in Egypt. They didn't have toilets, but tiled holes in the floor that people squatted down and used! Rose remembered how she and Camelia had rolled their eyes, and Camelia had yelled "Yikes!" so loud, her dad gave her a quelling look. Rose was still amazed when she thought of the bathroom without a toilet seat!

Rose's week of disappointments hadn't ended with saying goodbye to Camelia on Sunday. Rose had wanted to spend the next school week with the Hijab-Ez, especially Christina, but she had also wanted to spend the week with Fahd and Abdul.

Sunday evening, Fahd and Abdul had decided they were going to take a five-day trip to explore some historical Indian ruins at a place called Mesa Verde. It was near a famous location called 'The Four Corners.' The Four Corners is the only location in the United States where the boundaries of four states meet (Arizona, Utah, Colorado, and New Mexico). Rose had wanted to go on the trip with Fahd and Abdul. They would be going back to Saudi Arabia in less than two weeks, and she had wanted to spend as much of this time as she could with them. Grandma and Grandpa had agreed to take some vacation time from work to go on the trip, but Rose's dad had said she could not miss the last week of school.

Fahd and Abdul had promised to be back from their trip on Friday, Rose's last day of school. When Rose had gone to bed Sunday evening, she had still been just a tiny bit mad at her dad for not letting her go on the trip.

"Rose, we're at the school now," Grandpa said loudly to get her attention.

Rose shook her head as if to clear her mind and smiled at her grandpa. "Bye, Grandpa. See you after lunch," Rose said and hugged him. Rose walked towards the playground area and saw her Hijab-Ez friends standing by the wall, waving to her. Rose waved back to the Hijab-Ez, minus one.

—————— **5** ——————

Grandma's Secret

For Rose, the week seemed to fly by, like a fast moving train, a train without any brakes. The closer it got to Friday, the last day of school, the sadder Rose became. The last day of school was something all kids look forward to, and Rose was no different, but this year was different.

Friday, the Hijab-Ez spent most of the morning talking together and reassuring Christina that she would always be a Hijab-Ez. Every now and then, one of the Hijab-Ez would wipe a silent tear from her eyes. At lunchtime, no one ate a single bite. Even Ruby left the food untouched. They were just worn out.

Rose tried to cheer up herself and her friends by telling one of Fahd's now famous stories. It was about Prophet Job. He had many trials and never lost his trust in God. Even when he lost his home, his money, and his family, he continued to thank and praise God. Prophet Job was well known to both Muslims and non-Muslims, so each of the Hijab-Ez could relate to the story. The girls were sad because they had not heard from Camelia since she had left the previous Sunday. They were hoping Camelia's first email would arrive any day.

When the last bell rang, ending the school year, the Hijab-Ez, minus one, stood on the school office patio hugging each other until their parents had to come and separate them. It was going to be a long summer for Rose and her Hijab-Ez friends.

❧

"Do you want to go to the pizza place today?" Grandpa asked as he started the truck and pulled out of the parking lot across from the school.

"Nah, not today, Grandpa. What time will Grandma be home from work?" Rose asked.

"She didn't go to work today. Right now, she's visiting Sylvia at The Phoenician Restaurant," Grandpa replied.

"Ya know, Grandpa, Grandma has been going to visit Sylvia a lot. I mean, during the last month, she has been taking time off from work and visiting Sylvia during the day when I'm at school. She hasn't taken me with her, not once. Don't you think that's strange?" Rose said in more of a statement than a question to Grandpa.

"I hadn't thought about it much, but you're right. Grandma has been taking time off from work. She has lots of vacation time built up and unpaid over-time hours, too. I didn't notice that she was visiting with Sylvia so much. She hasn't mentioned what she does when she is with Sylvia," said Grandpa thoughtfully.

Hmmm…do I have a new mystery to solve? Rose wondered. "Is it okay if I ask her about this?" Rose asked.

"Sweetie, I know just how curious you can get, but I think if your grandma wanted us to know anything about her visits, she would have said something. Don't you?" Grandpa said this gently, but with a firmness that let Rose know that asking Grandma about her business was not something she should do.

Rose made a big production of sighing and then said sweetly, "Okay, Grandpa. I get the message loud and clear. I won't ask Grandma why she goes to The Phoenician Restaurant so much." *But I didn't say I wasn't going to snoop around or ask questions that might give me some clues,* Rose thought with her usual air of determination when confronted with a new mystery!

❧

Rose was busy sorting all her school papers in the family room. She made neat piles of things she wanted Grandma to place in the scrapbook she made for Rose each year. Beside the small, neat piles of schoolwork, award certificates, and ribbons was a huge, messy pile of papers Rose was going to throw away. Grandpa was supposed to be reading the newspaper, but Rose could hear him snoring behind the opened paper he held in front of his face.

The front door opened and Grandma called out, "Where is everybody? I need some help with the groceries."

"Coming, Grandma," Rose called back as she lightly swatted the newspaper Grandpa was holding.

"What? What?" Grandpa said. Rose grinned at him. Grandpa was always trying to pretend he didn't fall asleep when reading the newspaper.

"Grandma says to come help her bring in the groceries." Rose grinned impishly at her sleepy-eyed Grandpa.

"Be right there," Grandpa called out loudly and pulled gently on Rose's long ponytail.

Rose and Grandpa met Grandma at the trunk of her car. It was filled, or rather packed-to-the-max, with brown paper bags full of food items of every description.

"What did you do, buy out the entire store?" Grandpa quipped.

Grandma gave one of her pretend frowns—the kind you just know she doesn't mean because a smile always follows it. Everyone grabbed a few bags, and, after the um-teenth trip to the car and kitchen, the trunk was finally emptied.

"You haven't been moping around the house since school let out, have you, Rose?" Grandma asked.

"No, Grandma, I've been busy sorting my school stuff for my new scrapbook," replied Rose.

"That's my girl," Grandma said and gave Rose a big hug.

As they began to unpack the bags of groceries, Rose asked, "Why did you buy so much food, Grandma?"

"We are going to have a special dinner for Fahd and Abdul on Sunday. They should be getting home this evening, and I want to give them a day to rest up from their trip before we have the supper party," Grandma said and stuffed some veggies into the almost-full crispers inside the refrigerator.

Well, that was the shortest mystery to date. No fun snooping around or figuring out questions that might give me clues to what Grandma had been doing on her visits to The Phoenician Restaurant! She was probably having Sylvia teach her how to cook some different kinds of Arab food, Rose thought, just a bit crossly.

"No comments or questions about the supper party? I'm surprised, Rose! Hmm...why are you wearing such a ferocious frown on that sweet face of yours?" Grandma asked with just a little hint of her surprise creeping into her question.

Rose's face reddened just a little and she replied, "Sorry, Grandma. I was thinking about something else. Of course I'm interested in the supper party. How can I help?"

Boy, am I glad Grandma can't read my mind, Rose thought. *I wouldn't want her to know about my big plans to plot and scheme to find out her secret that really isn't any secret*, Rose thought.

"Let's see, I'm going to need your help with cleaning the house and, more importantly, help with cooking all this food I just bought. Excuse me a minute, Rose. I forgot something. I'll be right back to finish helping put the food away."

Rose watched as Grandma picked up the keys to her car and hurried out the front door. Rose stood behind the doorway and peeked around the corner as Grandma came back through the front door a few minutes later. She was carrying a large, white bag. Not the kind of bag the groceries were packed in. *Hmm...*Rose scratched the side of her head as she watched Grandma walk down the hallway to her bedroom and close the door.

Ah-ha! So, there is still a mystery to solve! Rose gleefully rubbed her two hands together and decided not to say anything to Grandma about the large, white bag. *I'll find out one way or another. I think that bag has something to do with Grandma going to see Sylvia all the time!*

Grandma came back to the kitchen a few minutes later and thanked Rose for finishing most of the work while she was gone.

She didn't mention the large, white bag, either! That was a sure sign to Rose that she was right. Grandma did have a secret, and it wasn't new cooking lessons with Sylvia!

∾

Rose and Grandma spent the afternoon putting together her fifth grade scrapbook. Grandpa went back to reading his paper, or more accurately stated, taking an afternoon nap!

Rose was placing the finished scrapbook on the dining room table when the front door opened, and there stood Fahd and Abdul with big smiles for Rose.

"As Salaam'Alaykum, our Little Rose," both boys said in unison as they set their suitcases down and walked into the dining room.

"Wa'Alaykum as-Salaam! I'm so glad to see you. I missed both of you," Rose shrieked as the boys each planted a kiss on top of her head.

"Where are Mum and Grandpa?" Abdul asked, just as Grandma walked into the dining room.

"Here I am, and Grandpa is taking an afternoon nap in the family room. I'm so glad you boys got back safe and sound. Did you have a good trip?" Grandma asked.

"As-Salaam'Alaykum, Mum," the boys said. "We had a very good time. It is most interesting about your early Indians and how they lived. Most unfortunate that your historians do not know why these Indian peoples disappeared from the area they lived in for so many years," replied Fahd.

"So, you did go to Mesa Verde?"

"Yes, and, Mum, we rode a train to a Wild West Town, too!"

"You mean you rode the Silverton Train to the town of Durango, Colorado?" Grandma asked.

"You are correct, Mum. We brought back, how do you say it? Ah…" Fahd paused.

"You brought back souvenirs," Grandma said helpfully.

"Yes, we did! We brought something special for our little sister. She will have to wait until the party on Sunday for her surprise," Abdul said as his eyes twinkled and his smile grew, while he watched Rose open and shut her mouth. She didn't even get a chance to ask any questions about her surprise.

Rose looked over at Fahd, hoping he might help change Abdul's mind about her waiting until Sunday. Fahd had such a tender spirit, but this time Fahd just shook his head. Everyone walked into the living room as Grandpa was shuffling the papers and getting out of his over-stuffed chair. Fahd and Abdul greeted Grandpa and they all shook hands.

"Have a good trip, boys?" Grandpa asked.

"We did, but are very happy to be home. We have to get cleaned up and go to the masjid for prayer, but when we return, we will tell you about the different places we explored," Abdul said. He and Fahd excused themselves, so they could get ready for prayer.

❧

"When can we go see the Indian ruins? Can we go there this summer? I want to take the train ride, too. That was so cool!" Rose chattered like a magpie as she worked with Grandma in the kitchen early Saturday morning. Rose was peeling potatoes and had the veggie brush and carrots lined up as her next task. Grandma was kneading dough for some fresh tortillas she was going to make later that day.

"Where did you say Grandpa, Fahd, and Abdul went? They have been gone a long time," Rose asked.

"I think that is the fourth or fifth question you've asked me in the last two minutes," Grandma said with a chuckle.

"You sent them to the market to get some more cumin, but that was a couple of hours ago. I think they must be having coffee and visiting with people at The Phoenician Restaurant," Rose said just a tad crossly.

"Poor Rose, stuck here in the kitchen, slaving away, washing veggies, while Grandpa and the boys are out having a good time!" Grandma teased.

Rose grinned sheepishly and continued to peel the potato with a little more vigor. "Are we going to decorate the house like Fahd and Abdul did when they cooked us our Supper Saudi Style? Hey, you didn't answer my question about taking a trip this summer," Rose sputtered.

"Number 1—I think we can manage to go on the same kind of trip as the boys and even take the train ride. We could invite Christina to go with us. Flagstaff is on the way to the Mesa Verde area. Number 2—NO, we are not decorating the house like the Nights of Arabia. Tomorrow we will sit at the table to eat. I am fixing every non-Arab dish the boys like to eat. They will be going home soon, and probably won't eat this type of food again, maybe not for a long time. Soon, they will be at home in Saudi and able to eat their traditional food every day." Grandma finished answering Rose's questions at the same time the telephone rang.

"I'll get it, Grandma. Your hands are covered in dough," Rose called as she grabbed a hand towel and went to answer the telephone.

"CAMELIA!"

Grandma heard Rose's loud squeal and the name Camelia shouted. *It must be Camelia calling all the way from Egypt. Thank you, God!* Grandma said to herself. Rose had moped about since Camelia and her parents had left for Egypt almost two weeks ago. Every day, she checked her email to see if there was a message from Camelia, but nothing. Rose was very disappointed Camelia hadn't emailed her as she had promised. Rose didn't have an address to mail a letter, either.

"Grandma! Grandma! It's Camelia. Their computer got lost from the airport and that's why she hasn't emailed me. They are getting a new computer next week. Judy says As-Salaam'Alaykum and hopes you are well," Rose rattled off Camelia's part of the conversation quickly.

"Go ahead and talk to Camelia, now. You can tell me everything after you finish your telephone call," Grandma called out to Rose, heaving a huge sigh of relief. Her sweet Rose would

96

be walking on clouds all day, now that she had talked to her best Hijab-Ez friend.

Grandma placed a damp cloth over the bowl filled with rising dough, washed her hands, and had intentions of joining Rose in the living room. As she approached the living room doorway, she saw Rose seated with her back facing the doorway, and heard the words "Grandma's secret." Grandma smiled and decided to do a little spying herself, so she listened to Rose's end of the telephone conversation.

"No, I told you, I don't know what is in the large bag. Uh-uh, she hasn't said one word. No, it can't be that! She showed me the two police watches she special ordered for Fahd and Abdul. No, I didn't snoop in her closet. What! If I got caught, I'd be grounded for LIFE! I'm going to try and ask some questions without actually asking her about the bag. When? This morning, we're getting a big, party supper ready for Fahd and Abdul tomorrow. Sniff, Sniff. Yes, they're leaving in four days. I don't know. I hope they write to me. Of course I miss you, but, well, they are like my brothers, the only brothers I've got. Oh, they are okay. No they haven't written yet. They all just left. Okay. I expect to see an email next week! Wait a minute and I'll get a pencil and paper so I can write the number."

"Grandma, I need a pencil and paper to write down Camelia's phone number," Rose called out loudly.

Grandma hid her smile and quickly brought Rose what she needed. "Tell Camelia to give my salaams to Judy, will you? Please remember to ask about her grandmother," Grandma instructed Rose.

"I did ask. The surgery went good, but her grandma will need lots of rest for the next month or two. Camelia says she is going to help take care of her grandma," Rose replied.

"Okay, fire away. Yep, I got it. Okay, I'll read it back. You sound just like my grandma! (Giggle) 1-999-010-488-949-4221. I miss you, too. Love you. Hijab-Ez! Friends forever!"

Rose hung up the telephone and turned to see Grandma walking back to the kitchen. Rose hurried to the bathroom and shut the door. She cried quietly for a few minutes. Everything was just so confusing!

I'm crying because I'm happy I just spoke to Camelia, and I'm crying because I'm sad we're so far apart. How can I be happy and sad at the same time? Rose thought.

Rose splashed her face with cold water and blew her nose loudly before leaving the bathroom and rejoining her grandma in the kitchen.

Grandma had finished the potatoes for Rose, and they were soaking in a large bowl of water. "Sooo, what are we going to have for our special supper party? I think I'll call it 'Supper American Style'," Rose joked.

"Let's see, your dad is going to fix tostados, tacos, and Italian spaghetti, with warm, garlic and butter, French bread. I'm going to fix roast beef with potatoes, carrots, onions, celery, and gravy. Then there's potato salad, refried pinto beans with cheese (Fahd's favorite smashed beans), and homemade, warm, cinnamon applesauce. Hmm…Grandpa is making their favorite scrambled eggs."

"Is that ALL? That's enough food to feed an Army!" Rose said in amazement.

"No, that's not ALL! I'm going to fix a nice green salad, some of my spinach dip with cream cheese, and I'm going to bake a tray of chocolate, fudge-nut brownies, and bake some of those peanut butter cookies Abdul likes. I think that's about it!" Grandma said with a satisfied smile on her lips.

"Do you think we will have enough time to cook all that?" Rose giggled at her little joke.

"Well, not if we both just sit around here talking about it rather than cooking it!" Grandma exclaimed.

Rose and Grandma grinned at each other, and it was then that Rose spied the sheet of paper on top of the breadbox. "What's this?" she asked.

"It's my list showing the order we are going to prepare the food," replied Grandma.

That's my grandma, always with a plan for almost any occasion, Rose thought, *just like me!*

At noon, Grandma and Rose took a break and had peanut butter sandwiches and glasses of iced raspberry tea out on the back patio. Rose gobbled her sandwich and spent some time playing with Taffy, Midnight, and Cappy. They had missed her during the last couple of weeks. Rose had been so busy she hadn't come out to talk with them.

Now would be a good time to ask some questions and see if I can get some clues about Grandma's secret, Rose thought as she scratched Taffy's silky back.

Before Rose had a chance to even think of a good question, the back door opened, and Grandpa, Fahd, and Abdul walked out into the patio.

"As-Salaam'Alaykum, Mum, Little Sister," the boys greeted them.

Rose and Grandma returned the greeting. Rose couldn't contain her happiness. "Guess what? Camelia called me this morning. Their computer got lost at the airport, and that's why she hasn't emailed me, and they are getting a brand new computer from the airport company!" Rose finished speaking in a rush.

"Subhanahu wa ta'ala (Glory be to Him, the Almighty)! You have good news, Little Sister!" exclaimed Abdul with a smile.

"*Radhi Allahu 'anha* (May Allah be pleased with her), I am happy your friend has called you," Fahd added with a twinkle in his warm brown eyes.

Grandpa just smiled at Rose and then turned to Grandma. "I am sorry we took so long. We met some of the boys' friends and one of their teachers from the university. We ordered coffee and before we knew it, the morning had just simply disappeared on us!"

"We were just taking a lunch break before going back to our kitchen work. Not to worry about being gone all morning. Rose and I already figured out that you would be chatting with friends," Grandma responded and smiled a special smile that was reserved just for Grandpa.

"Fahd and I are going to Mohamed's apartment. Mohamed and his family are leaving this afternoon for Saudi, and we

99

promised to drive them to the airport. We will return an hour or so after 'Isha prayer. The Imam and our brothers at the masjid are having a get-together in the community room for all of the Saudi officers to say, '*Fi Aman Allah* (May Allah protect you),' for our trip home."

"Please tell them we ask Allah for their safe journey home," Grandma said.

"We will say this," replied Abdul.

The boys gave Rose a pat on her head and went back inside the house. Rose heard the front door slam.

"When Fahd and Abdul leave, I sure am going to miss the doors slamming whenever they come and go!" Rose said and a wistful look crossed her face.

"When they leave, I'll have only ONE person to yell at about shutting the door and not slamming it," Grandma quipped.

Rose grinned at her grandma.

"Remember, your dad asked me to send you home after lunch, so you could help him chop the lettuce and tomatoes for the tacos and tostados," Grandma reminded Rose.

"Yep, I remember. I'll take our plates and glasses to the kitchen before I leave," Rose replied.

"Before you go, Grandpa and I have a couple of things we want to tell you." Grandma and Grandpa looked serious, so Rose sat back down on the glider and waited for Grandma or Grandpa to continue.

Grandma started with, "I have decided to retire from my work. I have worked enough time to receive a full pension each month and healthcare benefits. This means I will be at home full-time, because I don't plan to get another job."

Whew! I thought it might be bad news, but this is GREAT news! Rose thought to herself. She grinned and clapped her hands.

"Hold on a minute, Rose," Grandpa said calmly. "When your grandma retires, her pension will only be one half of the money she earns right now. She will get a check once a month. This means that we won't have as much money to buy treats, eat out at restaurants, and go on long vacations like we used to. Also, every time you go to the store, you won't be able to expect

Grandma or me to buy you everything that catches your fancy. Do you understand what I have explained about our finances and having less money?" Grandpa asked.

"Yes, I understand, and I am still happy Grandma is going to retire. She works too hard and it will be really nice to have her home each day. I don't mind about getting less treats and presents, either. Besides, there are lots of places we can visit and explore that won't cost so much!" Rose continued to smile at her grandparents.

This is possibly the best news I've had since the Hijab-Ez Summer Plan disaster happened a couple of weeks ago, Rose thought happily.

Rose looked at her grandparents and noticed they didn't look so worried. She stood up, went to each one, and gave them a big hug and kiss. "Don't worry about me. I know how to be very thrifty and I already shop for gifts at the Dollar Store, too. I can help by doing housework for FREE! You won't have to pay me anything at all, not even an allowance like you have been doing!" Rose offered.

"Thank you, Rose. I knew we could count on you to understand and help us make our new budget easier," Grandma said.

❧

Rose was so busy Saturday, helping Dad and Grandma with the cooking, and Sunday afternoon, spending time with Grandpa, Fahd, and Abdul at the park, she completely forgot about solving the mystery of Grandma's Secret.

Sunday the house smelled like a real bakery! The aroma of cookies, brownies, and fresh applesauce filled the entire house. Rose's dad had everything ready to heat up for supper, except the spaghetti. He was going to cook it when Grandma called, thirty minutes before they were going to start eating.

Rose listened while Grandma, Fahd, and Abdul discussed what the boys should do with their cars. They couldn't ship them back to Saudi—it was too expensive—and the cars were used cars (not new when they bought them). Grandma offered to sell them and give the money to the masjid on behalf of the boys. Fahd and Abdul said they had found a way to take care of the problem and Grandma shouldn't worry about it. "It's all taken care of," Abdul reassured Grandma.

That afternoon, Fahd, Abdul, Grandpa, and Rose went to the Park Lake to toss balls and feed the ducks. Rose loved to swing, especially when Fahd and Abdul took turns pushing her while she sat in one of the big swings. Today, they pushed her higher and higher, and she laughed from sheer joy. The boys and Grandpa laughed with her.

Rose, Fahd, and Abdul took a ride around the small lake in one of the paddleboats, which Grandpa rented for them. Grandpa decided to sit down and relax underneath one of the many shade trees surrounding the Park Lake and watch the young people enjoy themselves. Time passed quickly, and Rose protested mildly when it was time to return home to help Grandma get everything finished for the special supper.

When they pulled into the driveway, Rose saw her dad carrying a large table through the front door. "Our Supper American Style must be almost ready," she said as she got out of the car and followed her dad into the dining room.

Sure enough, Grandma was waiting to place one of her best tablecloths on the table. Rose paused in the dining room to smell the different aromas coming from the bowls and platters of food setting on the kitchen counters. "Go wash up and then you can set the table, Rose," Grandma said.

"As-Salaam'Alaykum," the boys said as they gazed at the banquet Grandma and Rose's dad had prepared for them.

"Wa'alaykum as-Salaam," Grandma replied and smiled. "Our supper will be ready in fifteen minutes."

Rose's dad left and returned a few minutes later carrying two trays of tacos and tostados. He went back to his house to get the spaghetti, garlic bread, and green salad. Grandma finished putting all the bowls and platters of food on the serving table. Rose hurried into the kitchen in time to get the plates, napkins, and silverware so she could set the table.

Grandpa came into the dining room just as Grandma placed a large vase of roses in the center of the table. Grandpa saw Grandma's frown. "What's the matter?" he asked.

"The flowers are beautiful, but there are so many I'm afraid we won't be able to see each other if I leave them in the center of the table!" Disappointment chased across Grandma's wrinkled brow.

"I can fix that," said Rose. She went to the kitchen cupboard, got a single flower vase, and filled it with water. She carried it to the dining room table, picked out a single yellow rose with a soft pink frame around each petal, and placed the stem in her vase. Rose took the large vase of flowers and placed it on the kitchen counter. She placed the vase with the single rose in the center of the table. "Sometimes more is not always better, Grandma." Rose shook her head wisely. "Besides, the yellow rose is called 'Peace,' and Fahd and Abdul always want peace for everyone!"

Grandma called Rose's dad, Fahd, and Abdul to come to supper. Rose's eyes gleamed, and her smile was as big as a huge watermelon slice, as Fahd and Abdul stood in the dining room doorway admiring all the special supper in their honor!

Everyone got a plate and began filling it with a spoonful of this and a spoonful of that. There were so many kinds of food to choose from that their plates were quickly filled.

After sitting down, Fahd and Abdul said *'Bismillah'* (In the Name of Allah), and Rose said a simple prayer thanking God for the food, Fahd, Abdul, and her family.

Rose kept a curious eye on Dad. She wanted to see how he would react as Fahd, Abdul, Grandma, Grandpa, and Rose were soon getting bites of food from each others' plates. This was the very first time Dad had actually sat down and had a complete meal with Fahd and Abdul.

How sad that Dad joins us only now, when Fahd and Abdul will soon be gone, Rose thought as she dipped a piece of tortilla into the spinach dip on Fahd's plate.

Fahd and Abdul were careful not to take any bites of food from Tony's (Dad's) plate. Rose whispered to her dad, "Muslims only use their right hand when they eat, and it is the custom in Fahd and Abdul's country to share food on the plates."

Dad smiled back at Rose to let her know he understood.

"After we finish eating, can you tell us a story, Fahd?" Rose asked with a winsome smile added to her request.

"After supper, Abdul and I have to say prayer, but later this evening, I will be happy to tell you a story, Little Sister," Fahd said.

Grandma had only put a very small amount of food on her plate. She quickly ate it, hardly tasting anything, as she was so nervous. "Excuse me. There is something I need to do. Everybody just continue eating. I'll be back, shortly," Grandma said as she got up from the table.

Just then the telephone rang. "I'll get it," Grandma said.

A minute later she called out to Rose's dad, "Tony, it was an officer from the prison. He says the Major wants you to report for duty right now. Some of the prisoners are getting out of hand."

"Sorry, Rose. Excuse me, everyone, but I must leave right now. I'll call as soon as I can. Don't be worried, Rose. You enjoy your supper and Fahd's story." Rose's dad shook hands with Fahd and Abdul, and wished them a safe journey home. Rose hugged her dad tightly and walked with him to the front door.

After Tony left, Grandpa, Fahd, Abdul, and Rose returned to their supper. Rose kept everyone smiling, as she told them her news from Camelia between mouthfuls of food.

"I wonder what is keeping your grandma," Grandpa said as he glanced at the clock on the wall. Almost thirty minutes had passed since she had left the table.

Meanwhile, Grandma was struggling to get dressed after a shower and shampoo. It seemed like it took her hours to get her thick, dark brown hair dried and put into some kind of order. With shaking hands and racing heart, Grandma put on her clean clothes and then her surprise. When she thought she was finally ready, Grandma sneaked a peek at herself in the mirror. Tears welled in her eyes, and she rushed to the box of tissues, dabbing at her eyes to stop them from spilling over. *Silly old woman*, she thought to herself, and then, suddenly, the anxious look on her face was replaced with a lop-sided smile.

Grandma squared her shoulders and walked towards the bedroom door. As she placed her hand on the doorknob, her hand began to tremble. Grandma grabbed her right hand to try and stop the trembling. Her shoulders slumped, and she managed to make it back to the bed and sit down abruptly, breathing hard.

I should have told Grandpa and Rose about my decision before now! Will they understand? What will they say and do? This is the most important moment in my life! We both talked about this, but he is still so uncertain. I have never been more certain of anything in my life! "God, help me now! Give me strength and the right words to calm their fears. Open their eyes to my joy! Help them see the light of truth! Amen."

Grandma stood resolutely and a calm serenity settled within her, like a warm comforter around her shoulders. She held out her hands and saw that their trembling had disappeared.

"Thank you, God," Grandma said softly with her heart and soul in these three words.

Grandma walked to the bedroom door a second time, placed her right hand on the doorknob, and turned it firmly, opening the door. Grandma seemed to float down the hallway and, as she approached the dining room doorway, she paused and looked calmly at the people she loved talking quietly together. Rose was the first to sense Grandma standing in the doorway. She turned her head and a look of astonishment flooded her face. Rose tried to speak, but no words came out. Grandpa, Fahd, and Abdul stopped talking and looked in alarm at Rose standing so still with her mouth wide open. They followed Rose's unwavering gaze and saw Grandma standing in the doorway smiling at them.

Grandma watched each of their faces. Grandpa's face registered surprise, confusion, and finally settled into a small frown that turned down the corners of his mouth and furrowed his brow. Fahd stood silently, with tears streaming down his face, saying softly, "Radhi Allahu 'anha (May Allah be pleased with her).'' Abdul's face was wreathed in smiles, and his joy radiated outwardly like sunbeams dancing towards Grandma and landing upon her smiling face.

Grandma walked into the dining room with her long, black abaya swirling just above the black stockings on her feet. The hijab she was wearing was a silver mist color, imprinted with large, pale, gold flowers, and with a very wide black band around the edges of the scarf. The hijab flowed down her back, and its wide corners crossed her chest and hung almost to her waist. Only Grandma's hands and face were visible.

Rose watched her grandma walk into the room with awe and excitement.

Grandma walked over and stood in front of Rose's grandpa. He stood up and looked at Grandma. Their eyes met for a long moment, and it seemed as if no one was in the room but them. Grandpa looked long and searchingly at Grandma. Neither spoke.

Rose was spellbound. She had never seen her grandparents so serious, and felt as though they were alone, apart from Rose, Fahd, and Abdul. It was like watching them through the other side of a glass window.

Their silence only lasted a few moments, but, to Rose, it could have been hours.

The silence was broken when Grandma quietly and firmly said to Grandpa, "I am going to take *Shahadah*, and I need Fahd and Abdul to help me say the words in Arabic. Then I will say the words in English, so Rose and you, my husband, will understand. By taking the Oath of Shahadah, I will become a Muslim, and will live the rest of my life as a Muslim in service to God. This is my personal choice. Accepting Islam as my religion is the right decision for me. I cannot wait any longer, because I know Islam is the truth from God, and I truly want to begin living in the way that I believe God wants me to live. I will pray, dear husband, that your doubts will be lifted and you will see the light of Islam as I have."

Grandma turned to look at Fahd and Abdul, who had remained standing, silently watching Grandma. "I am ready to say Shahadah." She gave a soft, encouraging smile to her Saudi boys.

Fahd and Abdul decided that they would say the words together, in Arabic, for Grandma.

"Ash-hadu an la ilaha illa Allah
wa ash-hadu anna Muhammdan ar-Rasul Allah."

Grandma repeated the Shahadah in Arabic, "Ash-hadu an la ilaha illa Allah wa ash-hadu anna Muhammdan ar-Rasul Allah," and then in English, "I bear witness and attest that there is no god worthy of worship but the One God, Allah. I bear witness and attest that Muhammad is the Messenger (Prophet) of Allah."

When Grandma finished speaking, Fahd and Abdul said, "Welcome, Sister Widad." Both Fahd and Abdul were smiling and crying at the same time. Grandma's face was lit up with her joy as she hugged Rose, Grandpa, Fahd, and Abdul.

Grandpa stood motionless and decided he would keep his jumbled thoughts to himself for right now.

Suddenly, understanding replaced the amazement, awe, and excitement that had chased across Rose's face from the moment she saw her grandma standing in the doorway transformed into a Muslimah!

So, this is Grandma's Secret! She wasn't at The Phoenician Restaurant learning to cook Arab food all last month; she was at the masjid learning more about Islam! The large paper bag must have had Grandma's new Muslim clothes inside it! Rose marveled at Grandma's ability to keep her secret!

6

Changes

Grandma, Fahd, and Abdul left to go to the masjid for 'Isha prayer after helping stack the dirty dishes in the kitchen. Grandma put all the food in the refrigerator except the brownies, homemade applesauce, and peanut butter cookies. When they returned from the masjid, everyone planned to have dessert, and Fahd was going to tell one of his stories.

After they left, Grandpa and Rose went to the kitchen and began washing and drying all the dirty dishes. They worked silently together. Each seemed lost in their own thoughts. They hadn't spoken to each other for several minutes.

Rose glanced at her grandpa. *He's so quiet. He must be thinking about something very serious. Maybe he's worried about Grandma being a Muslim.*

Grandpa often paused, while rinsing a plate, to stare off into space, not noticing that he hadn't put the plate in the dish drainer for Rose to dry. He had barely spoken to Rose since Grandma left for the masjid.

Rose was busy with her own thoughts, too. Since the first excitement and surprise of Grandma's secret being revealed so dramatically, Rose had begun to wonder about Grandma being a Muslim and what this would mean to her life and her family. So many questions were jumbled up in her mind that she was beginning to feel uncertain and confused.

I need to ask Grandpa what he thinks about Grandma being a Muslim, but he's acting kinda...I don't know...strange?

"Were you surprised that Grandma dressed like a Muslim tonight? Fahd and Abdul were very happy. I was totally surprised, but now I am a little worried. Did you know about Grandma's decision to be a Muslim before she told us tonight?" Grandpa didn't answer Rose.

I don't think Grandpa heard me talking to him, Rose thought, so she tugged on one of Grandpa's rolled-up shirtsleeves to get his attention.

"Grandpa!" Rose raised her voice, trying to get his attention.

Grandpa turned and barely looked at Rose's serious, upturned face. "Yes, Rose," he answered absently and continued to push the dishcloth around on the same plate he had been washing for the last minute or so.

"Yes, you were surprised? Or, yes, you already knew? Or, yes, to both questions?" Rose persisted.

"I'm sorry, Rose. What did you ask me?" Grandpa really looked at Rose when he spoke to her this time.

Rose rolled her eyes and said in a here-we-go-again sort of voice, "Did you know Grandma was going to become a Muslim tonight, and did you know about her Muslim clothes?"

"No, Rose, I didn't know anything about your grandma's secret surprise. I was very surprised! In fact, I was just thinking about this a minute ago," Grandpa replied.

"Are you happy or are you upset about Grandma being a Muslim, Grandpa?" Rose questioned softly.

"Right now, I don't know what to think about her decision. Grandma and I had many talks about how much she agreed with Islamic teachings, but she didn't say that she would be changing her religion. She didn't tell me she was thinking about doing this." Grandpa rinsed the last plate and grabbed a hand towel to dry his hands.

"Are you gonna change your religion and be a Muslim, too?" Rose asked.

"Let's go sit in the family room, where we can talk. I have a feeling you and I are going to play the game of twenty questions.

109

You will be asking the questions, and I will be expected to have the answers!" Grandpa chuckled and ruffled Rose's hair as she quickly tossed the drying towel on the dish drainer and followed him into the family room.

When they settled down on the couch, Grandpa pulled a white envelope from his pants pocket, unfolded it, and took a sheet of paper out of the envelope. "Before your grandma left for the masjid, she gave me this envelope. She asked me to read it with you. She said the note would help explain some of the changes we can expect, now that she is a Muslim. Grandma also said that we would sit down together and talk about this, later, when she gets home. Are you ready for me to read the note?"

Rose's eyes nearly bugged out of her head as she strained to see what Grandma had written. "Rose, I will read the note out loud, and then you can read it again if you want, okay?" Grandpa smiled as he watched Rose craning her neck to try and read the note.

"Okay," Rose said and smiled a little sheepishly. She settled back into the cushion of the couch and waited for Grandpa to begin reading.

Dear Ray (Grandpa) and Rose,

As I write this, I know you will be reading it while I am at the masjid after having revealed to you my "Big Secret." How I pray that you are feeling the joy of my decision and the overflowing love I have for my family at this moment.

I can just see you, Rose. You are sitting with your chin propped in your hands and thinking furiously as Grandpa reads this note aloud to you. You must have many questions. Some may be about Grandma saying regular prayers, five times a day, or maybe about when I will wear my hijab. Having Fahd and Abdul live with us this past year should help us in our understanding of so many things, like Ramadan and the Muslim Eid celebrations. I am sure you are wondering about what we will do for the family holidays we have celebrated in the past. Like I said, we will talk about these things when I get home, and, in the future, we will always discuss any concerns that may pop up from time to time.

Just remember that we are a family, and I love you both so much, as I do all my family. My being a Muslim will never, ever change this. And you, my dear husband, I know the struggles you'll be facing, now that I am Muslim. Together, we can work through them, just as we have done with every "bump in the road" during our twenty-six years together.

I look forward to returning to you this evening, having a discussion with both of you, and also having some of those double–fudge brownies that we made together, Rose!

Your loving Wife & Grandmother,
Lin (Widad)

Silence filled the family room as Grandpa's voice trailed away with the last words of Grandma's note. Rose's tiny sniffles began to fill the void, and her tremulous voice spoke the words she had been thinking, "Grandma is going to make so many changes... and my dad is gonna go ballistic when he finds out Grandma is a Muslim!"

Grandpa didn't answer Rose right away. It seemed to Rose that her grandpa hadn't heard her, so she tried to get his attention again. "But, I mean, what IF my dad is really mad?" Rose's voice squeaked and the worry she felt came out in her shaky voice. Grandpa shook his head, as if to clear away his unwanted thoughts, and he focused his attention on Rose. He watched the doubt and unease flicker across her usually sweet countenance.

"I will tell your dad that your grandmother, his mother, has the right to choose whatever religion she wants to believe in, and that will be that," Grandpa said with a good deal of firmness in his tone of voice.

"Then it's okay with you for Grandma to be Muslim? Are you gonna be a Muslim, too?" Rose asked.

"The same rule for Dad goes for me and all of our family. Each of us has the right to choose what we will believe or what religion we will follow. As for me becoming a Muslim, well, I don't know right now, Rose. Grandma and I have had many discussions about Islam, but I am not sure, like your grandma is. I need to learn more about Islam before I can make such an important decision like that," Grandpa replied.

"My dad says I can't be a Muslim right now, and I have to wait till I am older before I make any decisions about my religion," Rose announced with a frown.

"You must obey your dad and listen to him. Be patient with him, Rose, and give yourself some time to grow up a little more before you try to make such a big decision. While you are growing up, I think your grandma will be able to answer your questions about Islam. Grandma and I need to talk more about the changes she mentioned in her note. For now, I don't think I can answer any more questions. I don't want you to be worried about your dad, because I will talk to him when he gets home tomorrow," Grandpa said reassuringly and gave Rose a hug.

Rose nodded her head, but thought, *I don't think my dad will want to listen to Grandpa.*

"Do you think they will get home soon?" Rose asked for the umpteenth time.

"They should be home within minutes," replied Grandpa.

Rose went to the living room and pulled back the curtain, just in time to see the headlights of a car as it pulled into the driveway. "They're here!' Rose called out loudly and went to wait by the front door. Grandpa hurried to join Rose, and they waited together for the door to open.

Grandma was the first one through the door. Her face was glowing, and a beautiful smile reached up and lighted her eyes, causing them to crinkle up at their corners when she saw her husband and granddaughter waiting at the door.

Before anyone had a chance to say anything, Rose tugged on Fahd's shirt sleeve and said, "As-Salaam'Alaykum, Fahd and Abdul. Can we hear the special story now?"

Grandpa looked at Grandma, and their eyes met and held for a long moment. Grandpa then said, "Grandma and I were going to have a talk, but it can wait until another time. Right now, I agree with Rose. I am hungry for some of those brownies and I am curious about Fahd's special story!" Grandpa's big smile included everyone.

"As-Salaam'Alaykum and hello," Fahd and Abdul said.

As if on cue, Fahd said, "I am ready to tell my special story."

"Go on to the family room. I'll be there with the goodies, shortly," Grandma called over her shoulder as she began to remove her abaya and hijab scarf.

After Grandma brought a large plate of brownies, cold glasses of milk, and napkins for everyone, they settled back into comfortable chairs and the couch to hear Fahd's story.

Fahd began his story with, "The Story of the Green Birds of Paradise. Many years ago, during the time of the Prophet (pbuh), the new Muslims had many questions about how they should live their lives once they became Muslim and did not worship idols any more. They watched how the Prophet (pbuh) treated people and tried their best to have good manners like him. When they had a problem or disagreement, they went to him and asked for his advice. His companions memorized the answers he gave people. How the Prophet (pbuh) lived his life is called the *Sunnah* of the Prophet (pbuh), and the things he said and answers he gave people are called *Ahadith*.

"Years began to go by, and the people listening to the Prophet's (pbuh) teachings began to believe he was a Messenger of God. Those who believed became Muslims. This made the idol worshipers very angry. They got so angry, they tried to harm the new Muslims and even kill them. The Prophet (pbuh) and the new Muslims had to fight battles to protect themselves and their families.

"When a father, brother, uncle, even a grandfather died in battle defending Islam, they were called martyrs. The new Muslims were sad and worried about what happened to the people they loved after they died. The Prophet (pbuh) had already told them about Paradise, but they still had questions. The

113

Prophet (pbuh) explained that Allah had a plan for everyone's life and they needed to trust Allah. He told them when trials happened, they needed to pray more and thank Allah, because He would reward them if they remained strong when they had sadness and trials.

"The new Muslims were curious about Judgment Day. The Prophet (pbuh) explained that on Judgment Day, Allah will judge every person's good deeds and bad deeds. Some of the Muslims wanted to know what happened to people after they died, and what happened to people while they were waiting for Allah's Judgment Day. They wanted to know if martyrs have to wait for Judgment Day, before going to Paradise.

"The Prophet (pbuh) told the Muslims that Allah wants people to understand what could happen after they die. The Prophet (pbuh) told them that Allah made a plan for people and there are four parts to His plan:

"*First,* every person spends time inside their mother's womb before they are born.

"*Second,* every person is born. They may only live on the earth a short time, or maybe a long time, until they reach old age. During the time a person lives, they need to learn to love and serve Allah, do good deeds, learn how to fast and pray, give to charity, do acts of kindness, and grow in knowledge and understanding of Islam.

"*Third,* every person dies. When a person dies, Allah sends an Angel to take the person's soul from the body and put the soul in a special place until the Last Day, which is Judgment Day. This place is called *Al-barzakh,* meaning a 'separation or interval between the time of death and Judgment Day.' If you remain steadfast in love to the one true god, Allah, do good deeds, and pray, then your time in Al-barzakh is very pleasant. If you do not do these things, your time in Al-barzakh will be very unpleasant.

"*Fourth,* Eternity is where people will either live in Paradise or they will be sent to Hell. Eternity happens after Judgment Day. Allah decides who goes to Paradise. He is always fair and just. If a person does not deserve Paradise, then that person will go to Hell.

"Allah made a special plan for martyrs. The Prophet (pbuh) told the people there are seven types of martyrs in addition to people who are killed in Allah's cause. They are people who die in a plague, people who drown, those who die of pleurisy, those who die of stomach troubles, anyone who is burnt to death, any who are killed by a building falling on them, and a woman who dies while pregnant.

"The Qur'an says that martyrs aren't put in Al-barzakh. Allah places their souls in the bodies of beautiful green birds, and these green birds eat the fruits of Paradise, and nestle in the chandeliers hung from the throne of Allah. The martyrs stay in Paradise forever.

"The Prophet (pbuh) told the people that Allah didn't want them to be sad when someone they loved dies because, if they are good Muslims, they will meet them in Paradise after Allah's Judgment Day."

Fahd finished his story and realized that not once during the entire story had Rose interrupted him. *Perhaps she did not like the story,* Fahd thought with a trace of concern casting a shadow across his face. *Mum and Ray are sitting quietly and not saying anything either.*

Fahd looked over at Abdul with a question in his eyes.

Abdul understood and came to Fahd's rescue. "Did you understand Fahd's story? Perhaps you did not like it?" Abdul asked politely.

Grandma smiled and said, "It was a wonderful story, Fahd. We wanted to surprise Fahd and let him tell a story without us asking questions."

Fahd turned to look at Rose and saw her mischievous grin. "Thank you, Fahd. I really liked the story and it was very hard not to ask any questions, too!" Rose giggled.

Everyone in the room laughed at the joke Grandma and Rose had just played on Fahd. Fahd grinned and felt great relief. Grandpa shook his head and marveled at his wife and granddaughter. Both were trying so hard not to show their sadness because the boys were leaving the next day.

Abdul's voice became serious and he said to Rose, "Your grandma told us you were worried about Fahd and me because we are police officers. She told us you were feeling sad because you think we might get hurt and you will never see us again."

Rose's face took on a serious expression and she nodded her head solemnly and waited for Abdul to continue.

"Fahd and I could get hurt or killed doing our police duties, or we could grow old and then die. We trust in Allah's plan for us. We will try to live our lives in the right way, so we will have the reward of Paradise. During our lives, we will always struggle inside ourselves to do right. Muslims call this 'the inner *jihad*.' We will struggle to do well and help people. We call this 'the greater jihad.' And if we have to defend others, or fight for our rights as a Muslim, we call this 'the lesser jihad.' Fahd and I will be careful at our work, just like your dad and grandparents have been careful in their work. You are very brave for them, so you will be brave for your big brothers?"

Rose nodded her head and gave Fahd and Abdul a teary smile.

"Little Sister, there is something else I want you to understand. Do not get confused about the word 'jihad.' Islam teaches that if a Muslim has to fight, he must only do this in self-defense or to relieve oppression. Islam teaches that it is wrong to kill innocents or to commit suicide, and that a Muslim should not do any more harm than is necessary to stop something that is wrong. Do you understand what I am explaining, Rose?"

Rose's big brothers wanted to be sure their little sister understood. They didn't want to say goodbye to Rose with her being so worried about them and their work, or misunderstanding what she might read or hear about Muslims, but, most of all, they didn't want her to keep feeling sad for a long time after they went home.

Abdul looked over at Grandma and Grandpa, and they nodded their heads approvingly and smiled.

Rose got up from her chair, walked over to the couch where Fahd and Abdul were sitting, and she hugged both her big brothers. "I understand the story you told me and about being brave. I'll try real hard to not worry about you, like I do for my dad."

Fahd and Abdul both kissed the top of Rose's head and gave her a hug.

Grandpa had been quiet during Fahd's story and Abdul's explanations. He decided now was a good time to ask a few questions he had about Islam. While the grownups talked, Rose curled up on the couch between Fahd and Abdul, and rested her eyes. It had been a very long and exciting day. Rose wanted to stay awake, but her eyelids grew heavy, and soon she was sleeping soundly.

❧

Rose lay in bed and slowly opened her eyes. She stretched and looked around the room. For just a moment she was disoriented. *Where am I?* The last thing she remembered was listening to Grandpa talking to Abdul. Rose sat up in bed and scratched her head. *There's something important I need to remember, but what is it? My dad! He doesn't know about Grandma!* This thought jolted Rose awake, but her next thought was like a fireworks display going off on the 4th of July...*Fahd and Abdul are leaving! This is my LAST day to spend with them!*

Rose looked at the alarm clock. It was 9:00 AM. She hurriedly pulled on her pants, pushed her arms through the long-sleeved shirt on the arm of her recliner, and shoved her feet into her brown loafers. *The house is so quiet. Where is everybody?* Rose made a quick stop in the restroom and then practically ran down the hallway. When she got to the kitchen doorway, she heard voices coming from the back patio.

Rose opened the back door and saw Fahd, Abdul, Grandma, Grandpa, and Dad sitting around the patio table, talking quietly and drinking coffee. *My dad is here?* Rose thought in bewilderment.

"Why didn't somebody wake me up? I didn't know you had come home, Dad!" Rose stated indignantly to the five adults smiling at her. There they calmly sat, smiling at her, while a billion butterflies fluttered in her stomach, and she felt like she had just run a marathon race!

"Good morning to you, too," Dad and Grandpa said and laughed heartily. Three cheery As-Salaam 'Alaykums also greeted a now scowling Rose.

"Come give me a hug, Rose. Fahd and Abdul have been waiting for you to wake up. They are going to take you to The Phoenician Restaurant for breakfast." Dad smiled at his bewildered daughter.

Rose couldn't resist the five smiling faces. "I'm sorry, everyone. As-Salaam'Alaykum and good morning!" Rose added her usual sweet smile to her apology. "Did you eat breakfast, Daddy?"

"I got home just in time to have some scrambled eggs with your grandpa. Grandma, Abdul, and Fahd got up before the chickens. I'm kinda tired right now. You go brush your teeth and comb your hair, so you can go with Fahd and Abdul. Your grandparents and I need to have a little talk, and then I am off to bed to get some sleep," Rose's dad said tiredly.

Grandma went into the house with Rose to help her comb the bird nest from her hair and make two long braids. "Don't be worrying about our talk with your dad, dear. Everything will be okay," Grandma encouraged Rose.

"Do you think he is going to be real mad?" Rose asked with apprehension evident in her voice.

"Well, if he is mad, he will just have to learn to get un-mad, because I am a Muslim and a Muslim I am staying," Grandma replied firmly. "You run along now and enjoy your morning with Fahd and Abdul. Our discussion with your dad will be a short one because your dad is tired after working all night. Okay?"

Rose nodded and threw her arms around her grandmother's waist and hugged her hard. "I love you, Grandma," Rose whispered softly.

"I love you, too, sweetie."

Rose said her goodbyes to Dad and Grandpa, and left with Abdul and Fahd. Abdul called out as he reached the front door,

"We will be back about 2:00 PM. We need to run a few errands after breakfast. May Rose come with us?"

Grandma called back, "Have a good time and anytime in the afternoon will be fine to bring Rose home." She walked back to the kitchen, stuck her head out the back door, and said, "Let's go sit in the family room. It's starting to get a little warm outside, now."

Grandpa and Rose's dad followed her into the family room. "What time do you think they will get home?" Grandpa asked.

Grandma replied, "I expect they will be home in a few hours. When it comes to the boys, having a meal is not just about eating food—it's a social event! I'm sure they'll meet some of their friends at The Phoenician Restaurant." Grandma patted the seat next to her on the couch indicating to Tony that he should come over and sit next to her.

Grandma looked at her son and said, "So many things have happened rather suddenly in the last couple of weeks. Rose just finished the school year, two of her good friends won't be here this summer, and Fahd and Abdul will be leaving today to return to Saudi Arabia. This is going to leave a big hole in Rose's life. Even though I am retiring and will be at home each day for Rose, I am concerned that she will be very lonely. There is also something very important your dad and I need to talk to you about." Grandma looked at her husband and nodded her head slightly at him.

Grandpa looked quickly at Grandma and his son, and cleared his throat before speaking. "Your mother has made the decision to be a Muslim and practice the religion of Islam." Grandpa finished this blunt statement and let out a huge breath, relieved to have said the words out loud instead of the words bouncing around in his own mind! He looked anxiously at Tony to see what his son's response would be.

"What!" Tony's single word response exploded into the silent room, as he half stood up from the couch and turned to look angrily at his mother.

Before he could say another word, Grandpa stood up and placed a hand on his shoulder, pushing gently, causing Tony to sit down heavily on the couch. "Before you say another word, Son, I want you to remember something very important. Your mother and I raised you and your sisters in a home where there is religious tolerance and respect. That includes acknowledging that each individual in our family has the God-given right to choose what he or she believes about God. This means choosing what religion to follow and practice. Your mother taught you this since you were a small boy, and these rights apply to her."

Tony hung his head down and covered his face with his hands.

"I know you are surprised, Son," began Grandma, and then her voice trailed off as she watched her son shake his head violently, as if to push away the words Grandpa had spoken.

Grandma watched her son's anger and disbelief with dismay. She had known he would be opposed to her decision to be Muslim, but facing the reality of his rejection was so hard to experience. She clasped her hands to stop their trembling, and silently asked God to help her choose her words wisely when she spoke to her son. Grandma took a deep breath and said, "I know you are upset with my decision, but it is my decision. Being a Muslim will not change my love for you, your dad, Rose, or any of our family. I will still be your mother, concerned for your well-being, and will still be helping you with raising Rose. There will be some changes in how I live my life. I will need to rearrange my time so that I can pray regularly, my diet won't include any pork, pork products, or alcohol, and I think the biggest change for you and the family will be seeing me wearing hijab when I go out of the house."

"And what about our family holiday celebrations? Every year, we get together as a family to celebrate Christmas and Easter, Mother's and Father's Day, to name just a few! What about our celebrating Rose's birthdays! You always plan and have a big party for Rose and her friends! I don't think you are being fair to all of us. I think you are being selfish! God is God, so why do you have to choose to be so extreme?" Tony answered back with hurt and anger streaming from his voice and sparking from his green eyes.

"Enough!" Grandpa nearly shouted. His face looked like a thundercloud, and he shook his index finger at his son.

"You will speak to your mother with respect or you will keep your mouth shut! Do you understand me?" Grandpa thundered.

"It's okay, dear," Grandma said soothingly to her husband. She turned to her son and clasped his hand in her own. "I know some of the changes will be difficult, and will affect you more so than your sisters and the rest of the family, because you live right next door and they live far away. The changes will take some getting used to, Son, but you must understand that no matter what you say or think, I will be a Muslim. We can work together so that we can minimize any disruptions to your life and Rose's. As for celebrating your Christian holidays, I respect your right to do this. You have a home and can celebrate there. I will still enjoy family get-togethers, but will not join in with tree decorating or gift exchanges and such...but these are just small parts of our family get-togethers, right?"

Tony squeezed his mother's hand and said, "Okay, Mom, I'll try to adjust to the changes, but I don't agree with them. I won't like seeing you wear that headscarf, either, but I won't say anything, especially in front of Rose."

"Thank you for agreeing to try, Son. We'll work issues through as they come up." Grandma smiled at her son and husband. *That wasn't as bad as I thought it would be. There will be issues and disagreements in the future, but hopefully the worst is over!* Grandma thought as she gazed at the two favorite men in her life.

"I think I'll go and put on a pot of fresh coffee," Grandma said as she walked out of the room towards the kitchen.

"I am sorry for getting angry with you, Son," Grandpa apologized as soon as Grandma was out of hearing distance.

"I'm the one who should apologize. I guess I was just shocked when you said Mom is a Muslim. I think this is going to be like all the other times. Remember when Mom thought the true religion was the LDS church, the Mormons? We even went to church there for almost a year. Then, she studied with the Catholic Church. When I was in the seventh grade, she went to classes every Tuesday and Thursday night. And remember how she had the Jehovah's Witnesses coming to the house for over a year? Mom was probably influenced by Fahd and Abdul. Mom really loves those boys, and I have to admit, they are really nice guys. They treat Rose with so much kindness, and they are so respectful to you and Mom...well...I have to say that they changed my opinions about Arabs and Muslim men. I think there are probably more Muslim men like them," Tony said.

"I agree with you about Fahd and Abdul, and about most Muslim men being like them and not the fanatics that we see in the headline news all the time, but, Son, I think that this time your mother really believes she has finally found the truth about God. This commitment she has made is serious, and she didn't make it right away, either. It has been over a year since we first met Fahd and Abdul, and she started to learn about Islam. I really think your mom won't change her mind about this." Grandpa's tone of voice and facial expression were so serious that Tony paused, and his expression became serious again.

"Do you really think Mom will stay a Muslim?" Tony asked with a touch of fear edging his voice again.

"Yes, Son, I really think this is the last time your mother will go searching for the truth about God. I think she is convinced Islam is the truth, and I don't believe she will change her mind, not now, or ever in the future," Grandpa said with a huge sigh.

"Has she told Mona and Tina? What about my uncles? Uncle Chris is a Methodist preacher!" Tony exclaimed. His concern was reflected in his lowered voice. "I hope they behave better than I did, when they hear this news."

"Your mom has written each of them a letter explaining her decision, and some of the changes that will be happening because she is a Muslim. They will have a lot to think about, just as you and I do." Grandpa's tone of voice was gruff, and his face wore a serious expression.

"But, Dad, her decision will make a big difference in your life. Are you thinking about becoming a Muslim, too? Have you been studying Islam like Mom has?" Tony asked in a panicky tone of voice.

"I don't know what I am going to do. I am confused about some things I have read or heard your mother and the boys discussing. I need more time to think about all of this, and I need to know a lot more about Islam, before I can make such a serious decision," replied Grandpa.

"I have been too wrapped up in my job, and always relying on you and Mom to look after Rose. It's about time I started making some time for Rose. She's going to be so confused when Mom starts changing the way she lives here at home!" Rose's dad commented.

"You and I have taken for granted many of the things your mom does for Rose. You and I will have to be the ones to do the shopping for holiday gifts and the holiday house decorating, I think," replied Grandpa in a voice that reflected his dawning concern for the changes that would soon become part of their daily lives.

"Not to mention the big birthday parties!" Tony said and chuckled. It felt good to laugh, and, somehow, this broke the tension that had filled the family room and acted as a barrier between him and his dad.

Grandpa chuckled when he thought of his son trying to organize a group of giggling young girls!

Tony stood up and so did Grandpa. "We'll work this out somehow, Dad." Tony hugged his dad, and they shook hands as if they had just made a new pact to cooperate with each other in the uncertain days ahead.

Tony called out to Grandma, "No coffee for me, Mom. I need to get some sleep! Send Rose home after the boys bring her home, will you?"

"Sure thing, Son! I love you," Grandma called back.

"I love you, too," Tony said as he went out the front door and shut it quietly behind him.

———— 7 ————

Not Saying Goodbye

After Rose said goodbye to Dad, Grandma, and Grandpa, she followed Fahd out to Abdul's car, got in the backseat, and fastened her seat belt. Abdul and Fahd got into the front seat and turned to smile at Rose.

"Are you hungry, Little Sister? Abdul and I are so hungry we can eat a cow!"

"Silly, you mean eat a horse!" Rose giggled.

"But, never would Fahd eat a horse!" Fahd said with a poker face. Rose started to explain about cows and horses, but stopped suddenly, because she could see Fahd's mischievous grin spreading across his face.

"Oh, Fahd, you tricked me!" Rose exclaimed.

As soon as they got to the end of the street, Rose pulled her blue handkerchief from her pants pocket, put it on her head, and tied the ends securely under her chin. Abdul looked through the rearview mirror at Rose and smiled.

"Now you look like our Islamic Rose!" he said and smiled approvingly at Rose. Rose grinned and settled back in her seat for the short drive to the Phoenician Restaurant.

Rose licked the honey and nuts from her right-hand pinky finger and smiled impishly at Fahd and Abdul, who were seated in the booth across from her. "Yum! I just love dessert!" Rose said ecstatically and patted the box of baklava on the seat beside her. Fahd hadn't forgotten Grandma's special treat.

Sylvia, owner of the restaurant and Grandma's good friend, stopped by their table to ask if they wanted anything else. "We won't accept payment for your breakfast today! Everyone here at The Phoenician will miss both of you boys. Fi Aman Allah (May Allah protect you on your trip)."

Both Fahd and Abdul replied, "*Jazak Allah* (May Allah reward you)."

After their empty dishes were cleared away, Abdul asked Rose, "Would you like to wait in the masjid library while Fahd and I say prayer? After prayer, Fahd and I have a special surprise for you, and I want to teach you some easy Arabic sayings to help you after Fahd and I leave. You must promise us you will always listen to your grandma and follow her example. Will you do this, Little Sister, our Islamic Rose?"

Rose nodded her head and tears slowly slid down her cheeks. Rose's throat felt dry, and any words she might have said seemed to be stuck in her throat. She felt like her heart would burst. She didn't want Fahd and Abdul to leave her, but she knew they must go home and be with their families. Saying goodbye to Fahd and Abdul was going to be the hardest thing Rose had to do so far in her young life.

Fahd stood and bent over and kissed the top of Rose's head. "Come, Little Sister. We don't want to be late for prayer. No more tears now. We will see one another again, if not in this life, then, insha' Allah (Allah willing) in Paradise." Abdul and Fahd smiled at Rose encouragingly, and the three of them left the restaurant and walked quickly across the street to the masjid.

Fahd and Abdul left Rose seated in a chair in the masjid library with a children's storybook to read while they were in prayer. Before leaving the library, Abdul handed Rose a white envelope.

Rose put down her storybook and turned her full attention to the envelope Abdul had given her. Rose opened the envelope and took out a card. On the front of the card was a single blue rose. The words "Islamic Rose" were inscribed in gold lettering over the rose. Rose slowly opened the card. On the right side of the card, in Abdul's careful handwriting, were Islamic sayings, their meanings, and English translations.

To Islamic Rose,

When parting from someone: Say Fi Aman Allah = *May Allah protect you*
When a problem appears: Say Tawakaltu 'al Allah = *We rely on Allah*
When starting to do something: Say Bismillah = *In the name of Allah*
When unpleasantness occurs: Say Na'udhu Billah = *We seek refuge in Allah*
When pleasantness appears: Say Fa Tabarak Allah = *May Allah bless this*
When waking in the morning: Say La Ilaha Illa Allah = *There is none truly worthy of worship except Allah*
When you feel sorry for doing something wrong: Say Astaghfirullah = *I seek forgiveness from Allah*

I know these sayings (du'a) will help you, Little Sister.

Love from your big brother,
Abdul

On the left side of the card was a note written in Fahd's large and sprawling print.

To Little sister,

May Allah guide and protect you. Amen. I will pray for you each day and I will miss you.

126

Thank you for being my good friend and now you are my little sister. Think on my stories and not to be sad.

Love from your big brother,
Fahd

Rose finished reading her beautiful card and smiled. *I know my brothers will never forget me and I will never forget them. Even if they live a zillion, trillion miles away, they will always be with me!* Rose closed the card and looked at the lovely blue rose in the center of the card. The blue rose made her feel she was special.

Suddenly, like a thunderbolt, an idea popped up in Rose's thoughts, and she exclaimed out loud, "What am I doing sitting here!" Rose jumped up from the chair, walked rapidly across the room, and opened the library door very slowly and quietly. She poked her head quickly out the doorway to see if anyone was in the long hallway leading to the staircase that led to the upstairs circular prayer room.

The hallway is empty. Good! Everyone must be reciting prayers now! I'll just be quiet as a mouse and go up to the prayer room, walk around the outer walkway to the back of the room, and sit behind one of those big pillars while everyone is praying. Yep, I got on my scarf, long pants, and long-sleeved shirt, and my shoes are next to Fahd's in the lobby. I am going to talk to God and ask Him to help my dad not be so mad when he finds out Grandma is a Muslim. I am going to ask God to keep Fahd and Abdul safe all their lives and maybe find a nice wife for Fahd real fast because he wants to get married when he gets home!

Rose tiptoed down the hallway and quietly began climbing the steep stairway to the prayer room. As she neared the top, she could hear the Imam speaking. She quickly averted her eyes away from the large circular room as Camelia had told her Muslimahs should do, walked silently to the back of the room, and sat down behind one of the white pillars. *Whew!* Rose silently said to herself when she realized that no one seemed to have noticed she had entered the prayer room. When her heart stopped racing and her breathing slowed to about normal, Rose placed her hands on her knees and began her simple prayer to God. When she finished, she vowed that one day she would learn how to say prayers the Muslim way. For now, she hoped God would understand she didn't know how to pray like the Muslims.

Rose felt good sitting there silently listening and watching as the Imam led the sisters and brothers in prayer. Their quiet movements, as they bent in Ruku or prostrated themselves, were like the soft murmurings of a spring brook. It soothed Rose's sad heart and lifted her spirits. Gradually, Rose began to feel a happy sensation spreading everywhere inside her. It was like the trickle of rain drops on a window, slowly traveling their path downward to form a pool of clean, fresh water. This is how Rose's heart felt, all clean, fresh, and full of peace. Silently, Rose prayed again and asked God to protect Fahd and Abdul, and to help her become a Muslim when she grew up.

Rose sensed the prayer would soon be ending, so she carefully and quietly crept back down to the library. She didn't want Fahd or Abdul to know she had gone to the prayer room. They would feel they had let down her dad as they had promised never to take her with them to the prayer room. *Well, they didn't take me. I did that on my own!* Rose thought and smiled. She didn't like having to keep this from her dad, but he just didn't seem to understand how Rose felt about God and Muslims.

The library door opened, and there stood Fahd and Abdul smiling at her. Rose jumped up from the chair and rushed to hug her big brothers. "Thank you for the beautiful card. I will keep it always," Rose said with happiness brimming from her heart and reflected in her eyes and the beautiful smile she gave her big brothers.

Fahd and Abdul smiled back at Rose and then looked at each other with their eyebrows raised, as if to question the change in Rose. When they left her, she was a sad little sister and now she was bubbling over with happiness!

Fahd softly whispered, "Subhanallah (Glory be to Him, the Almighty)."

Just then a very tall man walked through the library doorway. He was wearing a long white shirt, and a round cap on his head. Rose was amazed and intrigued by this man's very long, dark beard and black hair that was sprinkled with white hairs, making his hair look like mixed salt and pepper! "As-Salaam'Alaykum and hello, Little Sister," the tall man said and smiled.

"As-Salaam'Alaykum, Brother Gamal," Fahd and Abdul said at the same time in reply.

Rose just stared with her mouth hanging open. *How does this man know me? I have never seen him before...hmmm...he called me little sister!*

Abdul solved the short-lived mystery. "Rose, please meet Brother Gamal. He is one of your grandma's Islamic teachers. If you have any questions about Islam, or if you ever need help, you can call Brother Gamal, and he will try to help you."

Brother Gamal handed Rose a piece of paper. On it was written his email address, website address, and home phone number. "I will be happy to help you whenever you have the need, Rose. Please give this information to your grandmother. I did not know until last week that the Grandma I have been teaching is the same Grandma that Fahd and Abdul mention frequently to me. I must go now. My wife is waiting in the lobby for me." All Rose could do was smile and nod her head.

After Brother Gamal left the library, Rose looked expectantly at her two big brothers. "No more surprises right now, Rose," Abdul said and he grinned a conspirator's grin at Fahd.

Rose looked at her big brothers and said unexpectedly, "You have made a good plan for us. I will be a good Muslim and both of you will be good Muslims. If I cannot go visit you in Saudi Arabia and you cannot come back and visit me, then we will see each other in Paradise!"

Now it was Fahd and Abdul's turn to look surprised. They had not expected Rose to come to this understanding so quickly. For the next ten minutes, Abdul and Rose practiced reciting the Islamic sayings Abdul had printed on Rose's card. When Rose told Abdul that she could remember how to pronounce the words, he gave her a satisfied smile, and Fahd patted her shoulder in approval.

"It is getting late and we must leave the masjid and take you home. We will be sad just a little time, and you will be sad just a little time. Then we will remember the many happy days we shared. We will write one another and call on the phone," Abdul said softly, struggling to keep his smile and not let any tears fall.

Fahd never struggled with his tears. He wiped his eyes and said, "I am the big babycry here!" Abdul and Rose burst out laughing and Fahd soon joined in their laughter. Sometimes he was just too funny! Fahd meant to say crybaby!

As soon as Abdul pulled into Grandma's driveway and stopped the car, Rose was out of the car in a flash and through the front door, calling out loudly, "Grandpa, Grandma, Dad! We're home. I have something to show you!"

Fahd and Abdul followed Rose more slowly and entered the front door just as Grandma and Grandpa met Rose in the doorway to the family room. Rose thrust her envelope and card towards Grandpa, and, without time for Rose to catch her breath, her next words rushed out. "Where's Dad? Here are your goodies," Rose handed Grandma the box of baklava Fahd had bought earlier.

"Your dad is at home, sleeping," Grandma answered and smiled at Rose's enthusiasm.

My, my! I expected Rose to be all long-faced and teary eyed, and here she is brimming with happiness! Grandpa thought and shook his head in surprise.

Just then, Rose remembered something very important. Grandma and Grandpa were going to tell her dad that Grandma was now a Muslim. Rose's eyes grew large and her heart seemed to skip a beat just thinking about this. Before Fahd and Abdul could even get their greeting said, Rose turned to her grandma and asked apprehensively, "Did you tell my dad? Did he go ballistic?"

Grandma smiled at Rose and gave her a quick hug. "Don't be worried. Your dad was not very happy when we told him, but he said it is my right to choose. Things will work out, just you wait and see."

130

"As-Salaam'Alaykum," Grandma greeted her boys.

"Wa'alaykum as-Salaam, Mum." Fahd and Abdul stepped forward and shook Grandpa's hand.

"Mum, we have a small errand to do. We will be back in a little time," Abdul said.

Rose looked surprised. *Where are Fahd and Abdul going now? We just got home!* "Can I go with you?" Rose asked eagerly.

Fahd shook his head and replied, "Little Sister, we have some business to take care of, but we will be back in two hours, not more. I am sorry you can not come with us."

Rose looked disappointed, but perked up when Grandpa said, "I need some help fixing your dog's fence. Would you like to help me? Maybe we can take your dog, Misty, for a walk?"

"I sure do want to help," Rose answered with lightening speed. She loved spending time with her grandpa, especially if they were going to be fixing things.

"See you later, al-li-gator," Rose called to Fahd and Abdul as they were going out the front door.

"After while, croc-o-dile," Fahd called back and laughed.

Once the boys were gone, Rose and Grandpa headed for Rose's house next door.

Grandma sat alone in her rocker chair on the back patio. Thoughts raced through her mind like a run away freight train. *There is so little time left before Fahd and Abdul will be leaving. I can't believe how fast this year has gone by and how far I have traveled. I am not the person my boys met a year ago, nor will I ever be that person again. Thank you, God,* Grandma silently prayed.

Grandma looked at her watch and noticed it was almost time for prayer. "God, please help me to memorize and learn to recite the prayer in Arabic," Grandma whispered out loud. Grandma was having a difficult time with learning Arabic, and her progress had been very slow with learning the prayer motions and prayer words. She felt so awkward, especially having to recite everything in English, except the few Arabic words she had learned from the boys! She had not memorized how to perform wudu' correctly yet, either.

I have so much to learn! Then there are my girls...what will be their reaction? Well, I already know my son isn't pleased. What if Mona and Tina and their husbands are upset and angry? My grandchildren will probably be confused, too! Do I have the strength to deal with their hurt? They will probably have many wrong ideas and assumptions about Islam, just like I used to have. Well, it is up to me to show them who Muslims are and what we believe...if they give me the chance! Grandma thought.

Fahd and Abdul paid the man at the car wash and then sat outside to wait for their cars to be washed and waxed. "One more stop after we are finished here and then it's back to the house to give our surprises," Abdul said as he pushed the sunglasses farther up on the bridge of his nose.

"Will you miss being here?" Fahd asked Abdul.

"I think I will greatly miss our little sister, Rose, and her family, and the many friends we have made here. Right now I don't think so, but I am anxious to go home. Perhaps once I am home, I will be missing our family here? This is a big country, and I would like to come back one day to visit Rose, Mum, and Ray. I want to travel to the many places we did not get to see, while we were here," Abdul replied.

"I will miss Mum most of all, and Little Sister and Ray, too! I am going to bring my wife back with me when I come to visit them. Maybe I will have children and bring them!" Fahd said with a hint of sadness, silent tears lurking in the corners of his eyes. Fahd grew even sadder as he thought about the years that must go by before he could return.

"Where did you put the papers?" Abdul asked abruptly.

"What papers?" Fahd pretended puzzlement.

"The papers we signed yesterday," Abdul said impatiently.

"You mean those papers?" Fahd grinned at Abdul.

"Yes, those papers! Where are they?" Abdul's voice grew softer when he realized Fahd was up to his tricks of teasing him again.

"I left them in an empty dresser drawer. I like dresser drawers very much. This I will miss when we get home. I could always find my clean clothes!" Fahd chuckled. "When I marry, I am going to insist we have dressers for our clothes!"

"Humph! You will be lucky if your wife doesn't go home to her mother, if you begin trying to organize her home! That is something I learned from my dad. He told me not to go making any changes to a woman's home, not unless you want to drink cold coffee and get the silent treatment!" Abdul advised his friend.

"Silent treatment? What is this silent treatment?" Fahd asked in surprise.

"Haven't you ever seen your father talk to your mother, and she just nods her head with an expression like her stomach pains her?" Abdul looked expectantly at Fahd.

"Ah ha! Yes, I have seen this, but I did not understand. Then my mother was not pleased with something my father said or did?" Fahd asked.

"Hmm, I am thinking of little sister and her famous word 'Yikes!' This is what is happening. So, if you want a dresser, I would put it in the marriage contract!" Abdul suggested to his friend.

"Excellent brother, thank you. I thank Allah for giving me such a good friend and brother!" Fahd said and clasped Abdul's shoulder in a friendly way.

"What will you do with all those books you bought? You have many books about astronomy. Also, Mum got you those Spanish cassettes and books. Will you still try and learn this language?" asked Fahd.

"When I get home, I will practice. It was too difficult to learn Spanish while learning English. Spanish will be easier because the adjectives are written after the nouns. There aren't as many exceptions to rules in the Spanish language as there are in English," Abdul said with an air of someone who knew what he was talking about.

"But who will you speak to, once you learn this Spanish?" Fahd said and shook his head in a manner that told his friend perhaps learning Spanish would not be of any good use.

"When I return to America, I will visit Mum and Ray, and then I will converse with Ray in his ethnic language. He will be very much surprised!" Abdul said and grinned at his great idea.

Fahd looked at his friend with respect and awe. *Abdul is very smart and he makes very good plans like Little Sister!* Fahd thought.

"The cars are ready. I will go and pick up Little Sister's surprise and meet you at the house. I will not be very long in doing this," Fahd said as he walked towards his clean and polished car.

Abdul called out, "I will follow you to the store. I want to get something else for Rose."

Rose kept an anxious eye on the clock, while waiting for Fahd and Abdul to return from their errands. Grandma finally convinced Rose to join her and Grandpa on the back patio.

Grandpa, Grandma, and Rose were playing with Rose's cat friends when Fahd poked his head out the back door and said, "As-Salaam'Alaykum. We have a surprise for you, Little Sister!"

Rose clapped her hands in her excitement, jumped up from the swing glider, and hurried after Fahd through the kitchen.

"I think we should go see the big surprise," Grandpa said and grinned at Grandma as they followed Rose into the house.

On the dining room table was a beautiful white birdcage with two green parakeets perched on a swing hanging from the center top of the birdcage. "Oh, they are beautiful. I've never had any bird friends before! Thank you, Fahd and Abdul," Rose said excitedly. She ran over to the boys and gave each a big hug. Fahd and Abdul hugged Rose back. Their huge smiles showed their delight in making Rose happy, and they stood grinning at her as she began to softly coo at her new bird friends. When Rose gently poked a finger through two white bars in the birdcage, the birds began to twitter noisily as if they were scolding Rose!

"Look, Grandma and Grandpa! Fahd and Abdul gave me two birds and this beautiful white birdcage that looks like a castle. They remind me of Fahd's story about the Green Birds of Paradise! Where shall we hang it? What should I name the birds? Do they already have names?" Rose's questions came in a rapid-fire succession, one after another. Rose was breathless; her eyes sparkled and her face shone with pleasure and excitement.

"Wait just one moment, Little Sister. Fahd and I have surprises for your grandparents, too," Abdul said with a glint of mischief in his brown eyes. Rose looked at the boys expectantly, and they smiled broadly back at her. It was only now that she noticed they had their hands hidden behind their backs.

Before Rose could question them, Grandma exclaimed, "You have a surprise for us?" Her anticipation was apparent by the happy expression on her face. Grandpa looked at the boys with raised eyebrows, as if saying out loud, "A surprise!"

Fahd walked over to Grandma and brought his hands forward. He was holding a piece of paper and his car keys, which hung on a key ring that had the name Mum written on a gold-edged tag.

Abdul walked over to Grandpa and brought his hands forward. He was also holding a piece of paper and his car keys, with a key ring that had the name Ray written on a gold-edged tag.

"Fahd and I decided that we would give you our cars. We know that you can use them, especially Mum, because her car is always breaking down. The papers are the titles, which Fahd and I signed and had notarized at the bank. We want you to have the cars as our small thank you for all you have done for us, and because we love you and appreciate how hard you have worked to make us feel at home in your home."

Rose watched as Grandma and Grandpa looked at the boys. Grandma had tears in her eyes and Rose was certain she saw a tear or two glistening in Grandpa's eyes, too!

"I don't know what to say. This is such a huge gift. Are you sure this is what you want? I told you I would sell the cars for you and send you the money," Grandma said softly, not quite taking it in yet that the boys had given them their cars.

"Thank you, Abdul. This is a very generous and kind gift you have given me. And thank you, Fahd, for your gift to my wife, also," Grandpa said as he stared at the key chain that had his name on the tag.

"Well, why are we just standing here? Let's go into the family room and visit for a while. What time is your plane leaving tonight?" Grandma asked.

"We must be at the airport by 10:00 PM, and our plane leaves at 11:30 PM. Fahd and I have asked the Imam to give us a ride to the airport, as it will be late and we do not want you to have to stay up to take us," Abdul answered with a gentle smile for his American mum.

Rose sat on the couch between Fahd and Abdul, and tried very hard not to feel sad. She blinked rapidly to stall any tears lurking and waiting to fall.

"How long will your flight be to Saudi?" Grandpa asked as a way to break the mounting tension he felt as he watched everyone struggle with their emotions.

Fahd cleared his throat and replied, "We will fly first to New York. This will be six hours. From New York, we fly on a plane from the Saudi Airlines, and this will take us twelve hours to get to our home. I will be sleeping most of this time. I do not like to fly on airplanes."

"Will your family meet you at the airport when you arrive in Riyadh?" Grandma asked Abdul.

"Yes, my mother, father, and many relatives will be waiting. We will travel to my mother's home, and she will have made a big dinner. She has said that all of our family and neighbors will be coming to the house to greet me and welcome me home. Afterwards, my father, brothers, and I will go to the masjid to pray. I will be very happy to hear the Adhan and pray with my family in our masjid. After prayers, we will return home, and I will give my family the many gifts I have bought for them while I have been here. I am most honored to give them the gifts you have asked me to give them," Abdul replied.

"Will your family be at the airport to get you, Fahd?" Rose's curiosity was running full throttle, now that Abdul had described his soon-to-be homecoming.

"My father and brothers will be at the airport to greet me. My sisters and mother will wait for me at home. My mother is planning a big party and she will be busy seeing to the many guests. My little sister may make big eyes and show tears to my father, and if this is so, she may be at the airport." Fahd smiled at Rose, and she knew he was teasing her because she had often made BIG eyes and shed a tear or two, to wheedle her way towards changing her grandpa's mind.

"How soon will you need to go back to work?" Grandpa asked.

"Our government is very generous. We will have a month to visit our families after we return. Many of the Saudi officers who were here with us have wives and children. They will need this time to spend with their family. Fahd and I plan to make a trip to Jeddah and visit his family's farm. We will spend some time riding the camels. I have missed riding in the desert and camping out."

"Will you take your telescope and look at the stars, Abdul?" *I remember Fahd telling us about the camels at his father's farm,* Rose thought.

"Another time, I will do this, Little Sister."

"Abdul will make me do all the cooking, while he is looking at the stars!" Fahd teased, and there was definitely a twinkle in his eyes as he grinned broadly at his friend Abdul, and then at Rose.

Rose giggled and said, "But, Fahd, you are not a very good cook!"

"This is so. Abdul will be most sorry if he doesn't help me with the cooking!"

The front door slammed, and Rose jumped up from the couch. "I bet that's my dad!"

Rose's dad walked into the family room. His hair was sticking up, his chin had sprouted whiskers, and he was rubbing the sleep from his right eye. "Why didn't somebody wake me up? I am glad I got over here in time to say goodbye to you. As-Salaam'-

Alaykum." Tony walked over to Fahd and Abdul, and stretched out his hand.

Fahd and Abdul stood up, and both of them smiled at Rose's dad and replied, "Wa'alaykum as-Salaam, Tony."

Abdul shook Tony's hand and said, "Fahd and I thank you for allowing your daughter to be such a help and a friend to us. Rose is a very kind person and she has helped to make our time away from our families much easier."

Fahd shook Tony's hand and said, "Thank you for the welcome to your country and family. I will not forget this kindness."

Rose watched her dad and felt pride and happiness fill her heart. She had wanted to ask her dad to come and say goodbye to Fahd and Abdul, but was not sure if he would want to do this. Now she felt relieved, and happy for Fahd and Abdul, too!

Grandma felt a surge of love and gratitude towards her son. *It will be difficult for Rose and my boys to say their last goodbye. I am so glad her dad is here to comfort her,* she thought.

Rose sucked her breath and choked back a sob as she grabbed Fahd and hugged him hard. Fahd hugged his little sister back and kissed the top of her head. "As-Salaam'Alaykum, my Little Sister, my Islamic Rose," Fahd whispered to Rose.

"Fahd, I love you, and don't forget me. As-Salaam'Alaykum," Rose whispered in Fahd's ear and kissed his cheek.

Rose turned to Abdul, who stood with his arms opened and folded Rose in a bear hug as he whispered, "As-Salaam'Alaykum, my Islamic Rose." Abdul kissed the top of Rose's head as Fahd had just done.

Rose kissed Abdul's cheek and whispered in his ear, "I am not saying goodbye. I'm going to pray to Allah that I see you and Fahd again. I love you, Abdul."

Grandma could not help herself as silent tears began flowing from her eyes. She covered her mouth with her hand to still the sob that wanted to escape. *I must be strong for Rose,* thought Grandma as she quickly brushed the tears from her cheeks and, with a great effort, smiled.

Grandpa put his arm around his wife and gave her a comforting squeeze, while blinking back his own unshed tears.

Rose's dad gently took Rose's hand and began to lead her towards the family room doorway. Rose turned and looked one last time at her big brothers and, smiling bravely at them through the silent tears she had not noticed, she followed her dad out of the family room.

Fahd could not help himself; as his own silent tears coursed down his cheeks, he bowed his head. Abdul stood stiffly with his hands clenched, trying hard to control his feelings as he saw Rose's brave smile. Suddenly, Rose broke away from her dad's hand, ran back to the doorway of the family room, and said clearly, "Fahd is a big babycry!" She turned and quickly ran past her dad to the front door, with her dad following closely behind her. He could her sobbing as she ran towards her house.

As Tony gently closed the front door, he heard his daughter's big brothers say, "Hafitha-ha, ya Allah (May Allah protect and preserve her)."

Grandma saw the sadness on her Saudi boys' faces and turned away, collapsing into her chair. She wanted to give them time to compose themselves and she needed a little time to gain her own composure. She knew how hard saying goodbye had been for Rose and had witnessed how brave she had been. Grandpa hugged Grandma again and whispered, "Would it be easier for you if I drove the boys to the masjid?"

"Thank you, dear. I think I want to take them and spend a little time at the masjid. Would you like to come with me?" Grandma said softly to her husband.

Grandpa sensed that his wife wanted some time alone with her boys, so he said, "I'll wait at home and say my goodbyes now." Grandpa walked over to Fahd and Abdul, gave each of them a hug, and then shook their hands. "Having both of you stay in our home and become a part of my family has been an extraordinary experience and a great pleasure. You and your families are always welcome. I learned a lot from both of you, and I will be praying that you have a safe journey home to your families. Please call us after you arrive and stay in touch if you can. My wife and Rose will miss you greatly, as will I."

Fahd and Abdul thanked Grandpa and both said, "As-Salaam'Alaykum, Ray." Abdul added, "May Allah protect you and your family. Thank you for being our friend." Fahd was so choked up he could only nod his head in agreement.

Grandma left the men to visit for a few minutes while she put on her abaya and hijab scarf. *Please, God, help me be as brave as my sweet granddaughter,* Grandma silently prayed.

Grandma returned to the family room and said, "I am ready to go to the masjid." Abdul, Fahd, Grandma, and Grandpa walked out to the car Abdul had given Grandpa. Grandma got into the backseat first, and then the boys got into the front seat. Grandpa stood in the driveway watching and silently praying to God that the boys would arrive home safely. As the car pulled out of the driveway, Fahd turned to wave at Grandpa. He said softly, "May Allah be merciful and kind and lead Rose's grandfather to Islam for his sake and Mum's sake. Amen."

As Abdul drove, Grandma chattered on and on, asking the boys if they had packed everything. Did they have their tickets? She warned them about being careful in New York, where they would change planes. Finally, Grandma ran out of chatter and sat silently until they arrived at the masjid parking lot. Grandma saw the Imam waiting beside his car. Abdul turned off the car engine.

Fahd turned in his seat and handed Grandma a white envelope with the names "Widad" and "Our Mum" written on the outside. Grandma accepted the envelope and carefully opened it. Inside was a bookmarker trimmed in the color of fresh green leaves with a gold tassel at the top of it. On one side, written in English, were the words of Al-Fatihah. On the other side were the words of Al-Fatihah written in Arabic.

"Abdul and I thought you might use this bookmark to help you memorize Al-Fatihah, and then you could place it with your Qur'an. Each day when you read Qur'an, you will see this bookmarker, and know Abdul and I pray for you and think of you. If we do not meet again in this life, insha'Allah, we will meet in Paradise."

Grandma smiled at Fahd and Abdul through the silent tears coursing down her cheeks. Haltingly, and with a voice overflowing with sadness because her boys must leave, Grandma said, "May Allah reward you two with good."

Fahd, Abdul, and Grandma got out of the car. Fahd kissed the top of Grandma's head and said, with tears choking his words, "We will leave you now, Mum. As-Salaam'Alaykum. La ilaha illa Allah (There is none truly worthy of worship except Allah)."

Abdul kissed the top of Grandma's head and said softly, "Subhanahu wa ta'ala (Glory be to Him, the Almighty). I will not forget you, Mum. Fi Aman Allah (I leave you in the protection of Allah)."

The boys turned quickly away from Grandma and walked with heads bowed and slow steps towards the Imam. Grandma made her way to the doors of the masjid, turned, and called out to them, "I love you, my Saudi boys, As-Salaam'Alaykum." In her heart, she echoed Rose's words, *I'm not saying goodbye. I'm saying peace be with you.*

Glossary

Glossary of Islamic Words and Definitions

A

Abaya—An outer covering Muslim women and girls wear over their clothes for modesty.

Abu Bakr—He was a Muslim and close friend of the Prophet (pbuh). He was in the Cave of Thawr when the Meccans were hunting the Prophet (pbuh) to try and harm him.

Alhamdulillah—All praise is to Allah (God)

Allahu Akbar—Allah (God) is the Greatest

Ant—The Ant is the name of a Surah of the Qur'an, an-Naml

Astaghfirullah—I seek forgiveness from Allah

B

Baklava—a pastry made of thin layers soaked in honey and different kinds of nuts; walnut baklava is Grandma's favorite in *Islamic Rose* Books.

Bee—The Bee is a name of a Surah in the Qur'an, an-Nahl. Allah created bees that make honey in many colors; honey is good to eat when you are sick.

Bismillah—In the Name of Allah

C

Camel—Al A'raf, Qur'an 7:40 tells us that people who do not believe in Allah will not go into paradise just like the example of a camel cannot go through the eye of a needle.

Cave of Thawr—A small cave outside of Mecca. The Prophet (PBUH) and Abu Bakr stayed there until it was safe enough for them to travel to Yathrib (Medina).

D

Divorce—Divorce is permitted in Islam. It is disliked and should be the last decision after counseling with family, an Imam, or marriage counselor. Divorce is not a sin in Islam. Children are not responsible if their parents get a divorce. They will still have their mother and their father. Their parents will still love them. Divorce is allowed for specific reasons in Islam. One important one is when the husband and wife are both unhappy with each other and cannot be friendly or kind. They should get a divorce, remain friends, and still help each other raise their children.

Du'a—A short prayer (supplication) to God. Du'a is not a required prayer.

Dhuhr—Noon prayer

Durango, Colorado—a tourist town in the USA southwest

F

Fa Tabarak Allah—When pleasantness appears say: May Allah bless this

Fi Aman Allah—May Allah protect you

Five Pillars of Islam—The five (5) principles of Islam that form the foundation Muslims build upon, with the Qur'an and the Sunna of the Prophet (PBUH), to practice Islam in their daily lives

G

Green Birds of Paradise—The Green birds are Muslim martyrs. There are seven ways a Muslim may become a martyr in addition to being killed in Allah's cause: one who dies in a plague, one who is drowned, one who dies of pleurisy, one who dies of an internal complaint, one who is burnt to death, one who is killed by a building falling on him/her, and a woman who dies while pregnant.

H

Hadith—The things the Prophet (pbuh) did and said and the answers he gave people as reported by the Companions.

Halal Cooking—Be sure that ingredients you use for making food don't have any alcohol or pork/pork by-products. Check the labels first, and if you are not sure, you can check on the ingredient in question by going to the Internet address.

Hijab—The covering a Muslim girl or woman chooses to wear that consists of a head covering and loose clothing to hide the shape of the body. The hijab scarf covers the hair entirely. Usually only a Muslimah's face and hands are not covered. Some Muslim women choose to also cover their faces. There is also an "inner hijab." Inner Hijab is a Muslimah's modesty, willingness to obey God, and pride at being Muslim. Hijab is a state of mind, how you think and act.

Hijab-Ez—(pronounced hijab-ease) is a word Rose made up to identify the group of Muslim and non-Muslim friends who joined together to support her hijab-wearing school friend, Camelia. A member of the Hijab-Ez is a girl who wears a head covering regardless of her religious beliefs.

Hijra—To move to another place because you are persecuted or people won't let you practice your religion. The Muslims and the Prophet moved from Makkah to Medina because of the hatred of the people against Islam.

I

Imam—Leader of a masjid, oversees the marriage contract
Insha'Allah—Allah willing
'Isha prayer—Night prayer

J

Jazak Allah—May Allah reward you
Jazaha Allahu Khayran—May Allah reward her with good

Jihad:
Inner Jihad—struggle inside ourselves to do right
Greater Jihad—struggle to implement goodness in society
Lesser Jihad—To fight in the cause of Allah; Muslims only do this in self-defense or to relieve oppression. Muslims are commanded not to kill innocents or themselves and not to do any more harm than is necessary to stop something that is wrong.
Jumu'ah prayer—Friday congregational prayer at the masjid. All Muslim men are required to attend prayer at a masjid on Friday.

K

Khadijah (ra)—The first wife of the Prophet (pbuh)

L

La ilaaha illa Allah—There is no god but Allah

M

Masjid—A building where Muslims go to pray in congregation; usually has a dome and minaret.
Mecca—The ancient name for the modern city today of Makkah
Mesa Verde—a southwest location in the USA where ancient Indian ruins can be seen
Modesty—Wearing a bathing suit to swim would not be dressing modestly because Muslimahs don't show any part of their body to non-family members except their hands and face.
Muslimah—Muslim girl or woman

N

Na'udhu Billah—When unpleasantness happens, say: We seek refuge in Allah.
Nikkah—a Muslim marriage contract

P

Pen Pal Party—website location to find a Pen Pal at www.weloveislam.com
Prophet Muhammad (pbuh)—Last Messenger of God

R

Radhi Allahu 'anha—May Allah be pleased with her
Reverted—when a non-Muslim takes the Oath of Shahadah and becomes Muslim; returns to Islam; all people are born Muslim, but as children are taught another religion or nothing about Allah.
Ruku—a part of prayer where a Muslim bends forward at the waist

S

Saft Turab—a small Egyptian town; English translation for the town name is Dirt.
Shahadah—Ash-hadu an la ilaha illa Allah wa ash-hadu anna Muhammdan ar-Rasul Allah. In English, this means "I bear witness and attest that there is no god worthy of worship but the One God, Allah. I bear witness and attest that Muhammad is the Messenger (Prophet) of Allah."
Shari'ah—Islamic law that comes from Allah through the Qur'an and Sunnah of the Prophet (pbuh). The laws do not change; they are fair, just, and include mercy. The Shari'ah is a legal system that expects Muslims to be honest and truthful. Scholars base opinions on the Qur'an and Sunnah of the Prophet (pbuh).
Silverton Train—a tourist attraction; the train ride will take you to an old "Wild West" town
Spider—The Spider is a name of a Surah in the Qur'an, al-Ankabut

Shirk—Worshipping other gods with Allah. Allah will not forgive this sin.

Subhanahu wa ta'ala—Glory be to Him the Almighty

Sunnah of the Prophet (pbuh)—How the Prophet lived his life.

T

Tawakaltu 'al Allah—When a problem appears say: We rely on Allah

The Four Corners—a location in the USA where the corners of four States meet; tourist attraction

Tortillas—round, flat Mexican bread

U

United States Constitution and Bill of Rights—founding laws the legal system in the USA is based upon.

Y

Yathrib—In the days of the Prophet (pbuh) the Muslims made Hijra to this city for safety. The name was changed to Medina, which means the City of the Prophet.

A Special Note to Islamic Rose Readers

I hope you enjoyed reading the stories about Rose, her family, friends, and the Saudi police officers. I enjoy reading books, especially when the story is good and I can also learn something new. When I read a book that mentions a recipe that sounds like it might be delicious to eat or read a short description of a place I haven't traveled to, I want to try out the recipe or learn more about the interesting place.

This is why I have placed on my Islamic Rose Books website each *Recipe* mentioned in my books. I also created *Interesting Facts* which describe the fun places Rose, family and friends visit and there are many links to other websites that tell you more about these places.

To get your free *Recipes* or to read *Interesting Facts*, go to the Islamic Rose Books website at www.widad-lld.com, click on Books at the top of the screen, and then below each book cover you will see the link words **Recipes** or **Interesting Facts**. Just click either one and you will be able to print out the recipes or read the Interesting Facts. You will need Adobe Reader, which is a free software program to open these Links.

I hope you find the Interesting Facts fun to explore and maybe you will try one of the great recipes I have waiting for you. If you are a young reader, be sure you have an adult help you when you try the recipes. The original recipes were provided by Linda Kingston a sister friend of mine.

Don't forget to read other Islamic Rose Books: *The Visitors*, *Hijab-Ez Friends*, and *Stories*. New books to the series will become available in the future. Thank you for reading *Saying Goodbye*.

Linda Delgado

www.ingramcontent.com/pod-product-compliance
Lightning Source LLC
Chambersburg PA
CBHW030107070426
42448CB00036B/451